**New Directions for
Student Services**

John H. Schuh
EDITOR-IN-CHIEF

Elizabeth J. Whitt
ASSOCIATE EDITOR

Understanding Students in Transition: Trends and Issues

Frankie Santos Laanan

EDITOR

Number 114 • Summer 2006
Jossey-Bass
San Francisco

UNDERSTANDING STUDENTS IN TRANSITION: TRENDS AND ISSUES
Frankie Santos Laanan (ed.)
New Directions for Student Services, no. 114
John H. Schuh, Editor-in-Chief
Elizabeth J. Whitt, Associate Editor

NEW DIRECTIONS FOR STUDENT SERVICES (ISSN 0164-7970, e-ISSN 1536-0695) is part of The Jossey-Bass Higher and Adult Education Series and is published quarterly by Wiley Subscription Services, Inc., A Wiley Company, at Jossey-Bass, 989 Market Street, San Francisco, California 94103-1741. Periodicals Postage Paid at San Francisco, California, and at additional mailing offices. POSTMASTER: Send address changes to New Directions for Student Services, Jossey-Bass, 989 Market Street, San Francisco, CA 94103-1741.

New Directions for Student Services is indexed in College Student Personnel Abstracts and Contents Pages in Education.

Microfilm copies of issues and articles are available in 16mm and 35mm, as well as microfiche in 105mm, through University Microfims Inc., 300 North Zeeb Road, Ann Arbor, Michigan 48106-1346.

SUBSCRIPTIONS cost $75 for individuals and $180 for institutions, agencies, and libraries. See ordering information page at end of book.

EDITORIAL CORRESPONDENCE should be sent to the Editor-in-Chief, John H. Schuh, N 243 Lagomarcino Hall, Iowa State University, Ames, Iowa 50011.

www.josseybass.com

CONTENTS

EDITOR'S NOTES

Today's college student population is diverse, complex, and ever-changing. With more than fourteen million undergraduate students enrolled in the nation's two- and four-year colleges and universities (The Chronicle of Higher Education, 2005), higher education faces numerous challenges and issues in serving a diverse population. It is estimated that by 2015 the number of undergraduates will increase to sixteen million. With each generation of college students, these individuals have brought with them their life experiences, attitudes and beliefs. Together, these experiences have shaped the culture among college students and have made each generation a distinctive group of individuals. Factors including social, political, personal, and technological have influenced the way in which college students viewed themselves, the college experience, and the world they live in.

In the last decade a lot has been written about the different generations of college students. The two major generations that have been written about or studied are the "Baby Boomers" and the "Generation X" students. The "Baby Boomers" are defined as the generation that grew up with the space race, the civil rights movements, Vietnam, and Watergate. The "Generation X" followed the "Baby Boomers" and witnessed the fall of the Berlin Wall, the AIDS epidemic, and the creation of the Web phenomenon (Oblinger, 2003). Since then, the landscape of today's college students has changed dramatically. Unlike previous generations, the twenty-first-century college student is heavily influenced by information technology. A major contributor to the rise of this growth is the arrival on campus of students born between 1982 and 2003—a group called the "Millennial generation" (Keeling, 2003; Oblinger, 2003). Unlike their predecessors, "Gen-X" students, the Millennial students possess different characteristics—they "gravitate toward group activity; identify with their parents' values and feel close to their parents; spend more time doing homework and housework and less time watching TV; believe 'it's cool to be smart;' are fascinated by new technologies; are racially and ethnically diverse; and often have at least one immigrant parent" (Oblinger, 2003, p. 38). In addition, the increase among older adults pursuing postsecondary education has become a national trend. With the increasing emphasis on globalization in society and the workplace, individuals are seeking academic credentials to certify them for high-skill, high-tech positions in the world of work.

The changing landscape of students enrolled in the nation's colleges and universities is a result of different factors. According to Carnevale and Fry (2000), the growth of undergraduate enrollment is attributed to five

NEW DIRECTIONS FOR STUDENT SERVICES, no. 114, Summer 2006   © Wiley Periodicals, Inc.
Published online in Wiley InterScience (www.interscience.wiley.com) • DOI: 10.1002/ss.202

possible factors: a rise in birth rates between 1982 and 1996, immigration, pressures on older workers to add to their skills, better academic preparation among high school students, and changing characteristics of families. These factors, taken together, introduce a complex dynamic for professionals seeking to meet the academic, personal, social, and intellectual needs of today's college students.

In terms of demographic trends, recent data show that minorities will make up much of the new growth in undergraduate populations. In fact, an estimated 80 percent of the 2.6 million new students expected by 2015 will be from ethnic minorities (Carnevale and Fry, 2000). Carnevale and Fry pay particular attention to the growth among Hispanics in the United States, both in terms of population and their participation in the K-12 and postsecondary sectors. The authors maintain that Hispanic undergraduates will account for about one in six undergraduates on campus by 2015. As a result, Hispanics will be the country's largest college-going minority population. This phenomenon and demographic trend has significant implications for higher education broadly.

Understanding students in transition is not an easy task. It requires that we have an understanding of what students bring to the college experience; that is, prior academic preparation or training, life experiences, and cultural experiences. Holistically, these experiences serve as a set of characteristics and events that will influence not only how these students perceive college but also what their ability is to navigate the college environment. Given the rich characteristics of today's college students, student services professionals are faced with growing challenges in the types of services and programs they provide in the areas of social, academic, and personal adjustment. The ability to provide effective services to students is directly related to understanding how these individuals were socialized prior to their arrival to college—be it in their prior learning environment (high school, community college, and so on), home, social context, or cultural context. In addition, all educational institutions are not the same in terms of structural characteristics, size, traditions, student characteristics, location, and culture. As a result, the converging of the two worlds can create a high level of anxiety and stress, as well as significant challenges, for students during their transition process to the new environment.

Although the current emphasis today has been to think about the Millennial student, it is important to acknowledge that the twenty-first-century college student may be a "Gen-X" student who has expectations of customer service, a "Baby Boomer" who is participating in higher education via distance education or e-learning, or a "Millennial student" who exhibits distinct learning styles and favors teamwork, experiential activities, structure, and technology. No matter the generation a student may be a member of, given his or her chronological age, the fact is that higher education administrators, faculty, staff, and student affairs professionals must rethink their procedures and services if they are to successfully meet the expectations of their complex student body.

This issue of *New Directions for Student Services* provides an overview of the many issues facing today's college students with respect to the transition process, from how college is portrayed in the mainstream media of television to understanding the needs of transfer students. Ensuring the success of students depends on many factors on a college or university campus. Each institution has a unique cultural context that will influence the daily practices and procedures that are implemented.

In Chapter One, Mary Stuart Hunter traces the evolution of the First-Year Experience movement, which began in the late 1970s. Hunter explores how the lessons learned about improving the first-year experience for students can be applied to a broader context in higher education. Specifically, she describes the characteristics of efforts that enhance the first-year experience, including the importance of understanding students, changing cultures, faculty and staff development initiatives, and the nature of teaching and learning. Acknowledging that educational institutions have different cultures and political climates, Hunter concludes by articulating strategies for reform.

In Chapter Two, Barbara Tobolowsky introduces us to how college is represented in popular culture. She explores the role of the prime-time portrait of the transition from high school to college in terms of academic, social, and personal issues, drawing examples from the series and episodes of *Boy Meets World, Felicity, Sabrina: The Teenage Witch, Buffy: The Vampire Slayer, Moesha, The Parkers, and 7th Heaven*. In her descriptions, she addresses how these portraits influence new entering college students' perceptions of the college and how some of these portraits perpetuate stereotypes about college experience.

In Chapter Three, Jennifer Keup addresses the issue of promoting new-student success and the importance of assessing academic development and achievement among first-year students. She draws data from both the Cooperative Institutional Research Program's (CIRP) annual Freshman Survey and the Your First College Year (YFCY) survey. The benefit of using both surveys is the ability to have longitudinal data for students one year out. The sample includes more than nineteen thousand students at 115 baccalaureate-granting colleges and universities. In her analysis, Keup provides a picture of the academic and intellectual development of first-year students during the critical period of their adjustment. She concludes the chapter by addressing implications for faculty, academic advisors, and staff about ways to enhance students' perceptions of their cognitive development as well as to empower students to pursue quality levels of engagement and participation during their first year in college.

In Chapter Four, Jaime Lester describes the population and demographic projections for higher education in the United States, with a focus on the Hispanic population. She uses California as a backdrop to investigate the transition of students from community colleges to four-year institutions. For ethnic minorities, community colleges are the schools of choice to begin their postsecondary education. In California, the transfer function has played a critical role in facilitating the movement of students from the two- to four-year college or university. Lester describes two programs that focus on providing transitional services and offers suggestions for institutions and student affairs professionals.

In Chapter Five, Soko Starobin acquaints us with the issues facing international students in U.S. colleges and universities. She begins by presenting a demographic profile of international student enrollment in the United States from 2001 to 2004 by student place of origin during three different time periods. Starobin discusses changes in policy and regulations affecting international students in relation to the growing concern about national security since September 11, particularly the implementation of the Student and Exchange Visitor Information System (SEVIS) and its implications for higher education. Within the context of racial and ethnic conflict around the world, the author identifies some of the challenges for student services to help foster a welcoming academic environment for international students and visiting scholars. She concludes the chapter with recommendations to academic leaders, faculty, and student services practitioners for developing and implementing programs to enhance U.S. students' understanding of international affairs in a global society.

In Chapter Six, Jonathan Compton, Elizabeth Cox, and Frankie Santos Laanan introduce readers to a growing student population in higher education—adult learners. The authors differentiate the terms *adult learners* and *nontraditional students* and provide national statistics of the characteristics and enrollment trends of adult and nontraditional students. In addition to reviewing the literature, the authors highlight exemplary programs at two- and four-year institutions that are successful in serving adult learners. Specifically, the eight principles of effective service to adult learners developed by the Council for Adult and Experiential Learning (CAEL) are presented. Using these principles, the authors provide examples of how six institutions have implemented successful services to these students. The authors conclude by discussing the implications of adults as students and their transitions as employees, parents, and students.

In Chapter Seven, Steven Aragon and Mario Rios Perez discuss the role of community colleges in serving diverse populations and how the transfer function benefits students of color. They provide an overview of the barriers to transfer and highlight some of the findings in the literature about transfer shock, transfer process, and transfer student recruitment. The authors profile a program at a research-extensive university in the Midwest called the Academic Year Research Experience (AYRE). One of the goals of the AYRE program is to facilitate the transition of freshmen and sophomore students in becoming actively engaged in research at the university. Details about the program, including eligibility, format, and benefits, are presented, with a specific emphasis on the benefits to transfer students.

In the final chapter, John Schuh and Frankie Santos Laanan discuss the impact of natural disasters on colleges and universities. Specifically, the authors discuss the concept of forced transitions and what this means for higher education institutions and students directly affected by unexpected natural disasters. Using the recent disaster of Hurricane Katrina, the authors provide a hypothetical situation about one student who may have been affected by the disaster. The goal of this chapter is to bring to the forefront some of the dilemmas, challenges, and implications for numerous stakeholders, including higher education leaders, administrators, faculty, and student services professionals, when faced with the needs of students during this traumatic event. There is no doubt that the colleges and universities in Louisiana, Mississippi, Alabama, and Florida are still grappling with the results of this disaster and that it will be many years before we as a society can understand fully the impact and scope of this event. In writing this chapter, the authors hope that the practical information provided here can begin to help student services professionals who work directly with college students develop and implement programs and services that will address students' transition and adjustment now and in the future.

The landscape of higher education is ever-changing. The students who are coming to two- and four-year institutions are becoming more diverse in every aspect, from their racial or ethnic background to the academic credentials and personal experiences they bring to college. Taken together, this diversity should be celebrated; at the same time, it poses challenges for student services professionals in meeting the needs of college students. The goal of this volume is to introduce contemporary issues facing higher education and to provide clear recommendations for practice and policy that can be implemented in strategies that are appropriate for the different institutional cultures and contexts. The recommendations are not supposed to offer a one-size-fits-all approach, but they are meant to give professionals the opportunity to make an introspective examination of their processes and procedures. The reality is that college students, new or continuing, will always be in transition. As a result, higher education institutions must continue to understand their students and develop programs and services to foster personal, intellectual, and psychosocial development.

Frankie Santos Laanan
Editor

References

Carnevale, A. P., and Fry, R. A. *Crossing the Great Divide: Can We Achieve Equity When Generation Y Goes to College?* Princeton, N.J.: Educational Testing Service, 2000.

The Chronicle of Higher Education. *The Chronicle Almanac 2005–06*. Washington, D.C.: *Chronicle of Higher Education,* 2005, *52*(1), p. 3.
Keeling, S. "Advising the Millennial Generation." *NACADA Journal,* 2003, *23*(1,2), 30–36.
Oblinger, D. *Boomers*. "Gen-Xers, and Millennials: Understanding the New Students." *Educause Review,* July–Aug. 2003, *38*, 37–47.

FRANKIE SANTOS LAANAN is associate professor in the department of educational leadership and policy studies at Iowa State University. His research focuses on understanding students in transition and the impact of community colleges on individuals and society.

1

Attention to the origins, history, and evolution of the First-Year Experience (FYE) movement in American higher education can inform institutional practices aimed at enhancing transition experiences of students.

Lessons Learned: Achieving Institutional Change in Support of Students in Transition

Mary Stuart Hunter

Today we live in a state of continual change. With each new academic year, we welcome new students, new faculty and staff, and new challenges. Our curriculum is constantly being tweaked, our budgets always seem to be shrinking, and the expectations for our productivity are ever-increasing. This, however, is not a new phenomenon for those of us who work in higher education. The fact is that transition is the condition in which colleges and universities exist. You would think that we would have empathy for students in transition, but do we? Is increased attention to students in transition evident today? Indeed, it should be.

A common explanation for increased attention to students in transition is frequently grounded in a desire to improve student persistence and academic achievement. Yet the motivations vary. Student-centered faculty and staff embrace sincere desires and altruistic attitudes toward helping students learn and succeed. Institutional leaders understand the very real fiscal cost of student attrition and the equally disturbing public relations consequences of unsuccessful students. Today's parents and families are more likely than those of past generations to blame institutions for their students' lack of success. And students, especially those who understand the ramifications of international competition in our global society, today desire programs and services to help them learn and succeed.

NEW DIRECTIONS FOR STUDENT SERVICES, no. 114, Summer 2006 © Wiley Periodicals, Inc.
Published online in Wiley InterScience (www.interscience.wiley.com) • DOI: 10.1002/ss.203

During the past thirty years, faculty and staff at institutions of all types attempted to improve the transition experience for students entering our colleges and universities. The First-Year Experience movement began in the late 1970s, gained momentum in the 1980s, flourished in the 1990s, and continues today. Many institutions have been successful in implementing change and reforms, while others have found frustration and disappointment. Much time, attention, and resources have been directed to the first year of college, and much has been learned. This chapter explores how what has been learned about improving the first-year experience can be generalized and broadened to provide assistance to higher educators interested in improving the postsecondary educational experience for all students in transition.

Factors Leading to Reform

A perfect storm was brewing in the 1960s and 1970s that led to significant changes in higher education and specifically addressed issues related to entering college students in transition. First, the massive expansion and widening of access to higher education that developed following World War II brought many more students to the nation's campuses. Many of these new students were first-generation college students. In loco parentis, which had existed in American higher education as an approach to student development since its beginnings, began to erode in the mid-twentieth century. College and university faculty stepped back from their responsibilities and authority over student behavior and development outside the classroom. A void developed. Dwyer (1989) identifies three factors that shortly thereafter convinced college administrators of the need for programs to help first-year students deal with transitional issues: students arrive on campus without student success skills; changes in curricula and regulations made decision making more complex for students; and the peer culture was no longer as effective as it had been in earlier years in assisting first-year students adjust to the collegiate environment.

Then, in 1984, a report entitled *Involvement in Learning: Realizing the Potential of American Higher Education* from the Study Group on the Conditions of Excellence in American Higher Education of the National Institute of Education (Mortimer and others) focused attention on the first year. The report's first recommendation was that "college administrators should reallocate faculty and other institutional resources toward increased service to first- and second-year students" (p. 25). Discussions ensued around this strategy, dubbed "front-loading," and the importance of the first year as a foundation for the entire undergraduate experience gained attention.

The FYE Movement

Attention to first-year students and the first college year had been developing from the early 1970s. The experiences at the University of South Carolina

NEW DIRECTIONS FOR STUDENT SERVICES • DOI: 10.1002/ss

provided a basis for increased national interest in the first year. Due primarily to the ideas of university president Thomas Jones, the work of program director John N. Gardner, and the assessment efforts of Paul P. Fidler, a first-year seminar program was created that showed promise for helping students successfully transition to the collegiate culture. The University of South Carolina assumed the informal role as the nation's clearinghouse for information on first-year initiatives until the establishment in 1986 of a National Research Center for the Freshman Year Experience on that campus formalized its role. Excellent work to enhance first-year student transitions has been done on hundreds of campuses, and the Center serves to help with the dissemination of research, scholarship, and information on programmatic best practices.

Early in the years of the FYE movement, it became clear to those involved in this important work that the first year was indeed important. But it became equally clear that the central issues were more about student transitions than simply about the transition to the first year of college. This led the leaders at the Center to rename it in 1995 to more adequately reflect a broadened focus and mission. The National Resource Center for the First-Year Experience and Students in Transition continues its leadership role in serving higher education.

Characteristics of Efforts to Enhance the First-Year Experience

A number of issues and characteristics central to the first-year experience movement are instructive and applicable to other educational reforms and student transition initiatives as well.

Importance of Understanding Students. Student attitudes, behaviors, and experiences are not static. With each entering class the world events and culture that shape their growth and development differ. Faculty and staff, however, sometimes tend to assume that the current undergraduate experience is similar to the experience they had as students. Attention to student characteristics, needs, behaviors, and experiences is central to creating and sustaining successful transition initiatives. Resources available to educators interested in better understanding today's students are readily available.

One amusing resource produced each year in September as new students arrive on our campuses is the Beloit College Mindset List. Compiled by faculty at Beloit College in Wisconsin each fall, this list describes the particular view of the world of each new generation of students. The list identifies some facts of life that distinguish each entering class from those that preceded it. "One of its primary purposes has been," in the words of co-editor Tom McBride, Keefer Professor of the Humanities at the Wisconsin liberal arts college, "an attempt to slow the onset of 'hardening of the references' experienced by some faculty" (http://www.beloit.edu/~pubaff/mindset/, August 10, 2005).

NEW DIRECTIONS FOR STUDENT SERVICES • DOI: 10.1002/ss

The Higher Education Research Institute at UCLA continues its annual survey research on student experiences, attitudes, and behaviors as it has done for more than thirty-five years. The Cooperative Institutional Research Program (CIRP) is the nation's largest and oldest empirical study of higher education, involving data on some 1,800 institutions and more than eleven million students. It is regarded as the most comprehensive source of information on college students in the country. The annual report of the Freshman Survey provides normative data on each year's entering college students (http://www.gseis.ucla.edu/heri/cirp.html, August 10, 2005).

The Your First College Year Survey is designed specifically to assess the academic and personal development of students over the first year of college. This survey enables institutions to identify features of the first year that encourage student learning, involvement, satisfaction, retention, and success, thereby enhancing first-year programs and retention strategies at campuses across the country (http://www.gseis.ucla.edu/heri/yfcy/, August 10, 2005).

The National Survey of Student Engagement (NSSE) is another nationally administered survey instrument valuable for better understanding students. This survey obtains information from colleges and universities about student participation in programs and activities that institutions provide for student learning and personal development. The results provide an estimate of how undergraduates spend their time and what they gain from attending college. Survey items on the College Student Report represent empirically confirmed good practices in undergraduate education. That is, they reflect behaviors by students and institutions that are associated with desired outcomes (http://www.indiana.edu/~nsse/html/quick_facts.htm, August 10, 2005).

An often-untapped source of information about students is also readily available on every campus. Admissions offices have abundant demographic information about incoming first-year and transfer students and offices of institutional research and assessment have ample information on students as well. Unfortunately, often this information simply sits on a shelf or on a computer hard drive and is not used to its full potential.

Changing Cultures. Another key ingredient in successful transition programs is recognition that students in transition are frequently moving from one cultural environment to another. Colleges and universities are no different from other complex organizations. Large corporations and the military recognize that in order to produce effective managers and service members, they must invest significant resources into management training and basic training. Simple osmosis will not transform new employees and members of the armed forces, so it is unreasonable for educators to expect osmosis to convert new students into successful ones. The days of the "let them sink or swim" attitude of faculty and staff toward new students are obsolete. Deliberate and intentional efforts to assimilate new students into the institutional culture and environment are essential if institutions are to expect transitional students to thrive.

Faculty and Staff Development Initiatives. Another element central to the FYE movement that is appropriate for transition initiatives of all types is that of deliberate and focused faculty and staff development. Traditional graduate training for faculty rarely includes courses on teaching pedagogy. Future faculty members are trained in graduate schools in a highly focused discipline. Those who choose to teach at the collegiate level are indeed experts in a content area, but they are not necessarily well prepared to teach effectively. Since the early days of FYE initiatives to prepare instructors to teach first-year seminars and other courses in learning communities, faculty preparation workshops and faculty development have been central features. Such training and development programs include a focus on student characteristics and demographics, active learning teaching pedagogies, resource development, and evaluation and assessment techniques.

The Nature of Teaching and Learning. Learning in the twenty-first century is far different than it was in years past. New technologies enable dramatically different building blocks of teaching and learning. Classrooms are no longer bound by four walls, books are no longer confined to pages in a binding, research materials are no longer limited to the institution's library holdings, office hours now can extend electronically beyond the traditional nine-to-five work day. Successful transition initiatives embrace these new realities rather than ignore them.

Teaching and learning once considered the private turf of the faculty and the classroom has broadened to a more widely shared endeavor. Several important documents published over the past decade provide ample food for thought related to enhancing students' learning and success within the greater higher education community. In a publication titled *The Student Learning Imperative: Implications for Student Affairs* (American College Personnel Association, 1996), the authors opened an important philosophical discussion on a needed shift in the focus of student affairs professionals to align with the primary academic missions of the institutions in which they serve. *Learning Reconsidered: A Campus-Wide Focus on the Student Experience* (Keeling and others, 2004), copublished by the American College Personnel Association and the National Association of Student Personnel Administrators, argues for the integrated use of all of higher education's resources in the education and preparation of the whole student. And, in 2002, *Greater Expectations: A New Vision for Learning as a Nation Goes to College* (Association of American Colleges and Universities) called for a reexamination of "what we should expect from, and how we should provide, college education in the twenty-first century" (p. iv). The document challenges stakeholders to adopt unifying collective actions to create an educational system that will help all students achieve greater expectations. These important reports and publications provide support for the creation of programs and initiatives designed to assist students in transition as they navigate undergraduate waters.

NEW DIRECTIONS FOR STUDENT SERVICES • DOI: 10.1002/ss

Strategies for Reform

Educators interested in implementing educational reform can employ strategies used successfully by educators working to enhance the first college year. Although each institutional culture and political climate will dictate strategies that will prove successful, much can also be learned from those who have plowed the same type of field before.

Learn from Others' Experiences. The inaugural issue of the *Journal of the Freshman Year Experience* (now named the *Journal of the First-Year Experience and Students in Transition*) in 1989 contained an article describing the theories and practices surrounding the politics of curriculum reform used while establishing a new seminar course at a Canadian institution (Smitheram, 1989). Smitheram's step-by-step guide is applicable to other educational reform as well, specifically reform involved in creating programs, courses, or initiatives for students in transition. His attention to sources of institutional conflict and obstacles to reform is instructive. The process he outlines can be adapted to reform of many types, and it details such useful suggestions as the following: selecting capable initiators; clarifying goals; defining parameters of a broad plan; building a coalition by employing a pragmatic political strategy, a professional expertise strategy, or a consultative strategy; attending to task orientation; and facing objections.

Relate Efforts to Institutional Problems or Situations. Determine how attention to students in transition will improve the institution or enhance student success. Be specific in addressing institutional problems or specific situations on campus. Detail the positive outcomes that can potentially affect students and the institution.

Link Efforts to Institutional Mission. For any educational reform to succeed on a given campus, it must be consistent with the mission of the institution. Every regionally accredited institution must have a mission statement that guides the institution. The mission statement, therefore, is the starting point in educational reform. A proposal for a new initiative for students in transition that is supported by the mission of the institution is far more likely to find success than is one that is counter to or outside of the institutional mission. A review of the verbiage of the institution's mission statement can also help in taking a general idea for a new initiative to a more concrete form.

Seek Support from Institutional Leadership. Be very intentional about tying efforts to institutional mission and priorities. Support and endorsement from institutional leaders are more easily obtained when doing so. With support from the very top level of institutional leadership, success is more likely.

Create Partnerships. Collegial partnerships between academic and student affairs benefit all involved. Many of the most successful educational reforms of recent years involve such a partnership. First-year seminars, learning communities, and residential colleges are three prime examples. New initiatives on behalf of students in transition will be more successful if they are broad enough and comprehensive enough to involve both the interests of faculty and academic affairs officers and those of student affairs professionals.

Form a Diverse Planning Group. A task force or committee with varying viewpoints is advised. Although a diverse planning group may slow progress initially, having all stakeholders represented at the table will result in a better and more comprehensive final product. Consider including those who are philosophically in step with the idea as well as those who will ask challenging questions and serve as devil's advocates. Include representation from all offices and programs that will have any significant interaction with the students involved with the new initiative. Because credible proponents for reform are a necessity, include campus opinion leaders and early adopters. Involve those who are known for getting things done. Do not forget to involve student representation.

Embrace Openness and Communication. Seek opportunities to let the campus community know about the new initiative. Positive momentum may be created, and others interested in the topic can contribute to the work of the committee. Campuswide communication will also bring out the detractors early and their concerns can be addressed during the development stages.

Incorporate Learning Outcomes. Beginning with an end in mind will help to guide development of a new initiative. Crafting observable, measurable, and attainable learning objectives will strengthen the initiative from the very beginning. Suskie (2004) defines a learning outcome or goal as "the knowledge, skills, attitudes, and habits of mind that students take with them from a learning experience" (p. 75). Assessing learning is key to getting results. In describing the assessment of student learning, Suskie suggests a four-step continuous cycle to guide assessment efforts: establish learning goals, provide learning activities, assess student learning, and use the results.

Plan for Program Assessment. Program assessment is critical to the initial success as well as the longevity of educational initiatives. Swing (2001) suggests that "programs that survive and thrive likely share a common link—a strong outcome assessment agenda that is closely connected to program goals," and continues by stating that "assessment findings can provide protection and leverage in hard times and guidance for improvement anytime" (p. ix). Planning for program assessment as the program is developed will make implementing an assessment plan much easier than attempting to layer an assessment over an established program. Regularly scheduled and self-initiated program review that folds results back into program improvement will increase the chances of program longevity and ensure continuous improvement.

Seek Feedback on Initial Drafts. Circulate early drafts of a program prospectus to stakeholding groups and individuals. Seek feedback, input, and specific suggestions. Then refine the proposal, incorporating as much of the feedback as is possible.

Start Small. Many a good idea has failed because it became unwieldy. Beginning with a pilot project on a manageable scale is highly recommended. Doing so will enhance the chances for success. Choosing outstanding faculty and staff for the program will also enhance the chances for early success. It will also enable needed changes to be more easily made as the program continues. Multiple measures for assessment are easier on a smaller scale, and results can be more easily used to inform practice.

Conclusion

The state of continual change in which higher educators work is both challenging and invigorating. Many opportunities exist to engage in reform efforts that will improve student learning and enhance institutional effectiveness. Having a sincere desire to create new initiatives for students in transition is admirable, but desire alone is insufficient. Learning from past experiences of other educational reform efforts can be useful. The lessons learned from those engaged in the First-Year Experience movement during the latter half of the twentieth century in American higher education can be instructive to those engaging in efforts on behalf of students in other transitions. Considering student characteristics and needs, understanding institutional cultures, creating cross-campus partnerships, incorporating faculty and staff development initiatives, linking efforts to institutional mission, and attending to the campus political process can increase the likelihood that new initiatives for students in transition will be successful. Although much can be learned from earlier initiatives at other institutions, perhaps the most important learning will be by those actively engaged. We must not forget that colleges and universities are places for faculty and staff to learn as well.

References

American College Personnel Association. *The Student Learning Imperative: Implications for Student Affairs.* Washington, D.C.: American College Personnel Association, 1996.

Association of American Colleges and Universities. *Greater Expectations: A New Vision for Learning as a Nation Goes to College.* Washington, D.C.: Association of American Colleges and Universities, 2002.

Dwyer, J. O. "A Historical Look at the Freshman Year Experience." In M. L. Upcraft, J. N. Gardner, and Associates (eds.), *The Freshman Year Experience: Helping Students Survive and Succeed in College.* San Francisco: Jossey-Bass, 1989.

Keeling, R. P., and others (eds.). *Learning Reconsidered: A Campus-Wide Focus on the Student Experience.* Washington, D.C.: American College Personnel Association and the National Association of Student Personnel Administrators, 2004.

Mortimer, K. P., and others. *Involvement in Learning: Realizing the Potential of American Higher Education.* Washington, D.C.: Study Group on the Conditions of Excellence in American Higher Education. U.S. Department of Education, 1984.

Smitheram, V. "The Politics of Persuasion: Establishing a New Freshman Seminar with Full Academic Credit." *Journal of the Freshman Year Experience,* 1989, 1(1), 79–94.

Suskie, L. *Assessing Student Learning: A Common Sense Guide.* Bolton, Mass.: Anker, 2004.
Swing, R. L. (ed.). *Proving and Improving: Strategies for Assessing the First College Year* (monograph number 33). Columbia, S.C.: National Resource Center for the First-Year Experience and Students in Transition, University of South Carolina, 2001.

MARY STUART HUNTER *is director of the National Resource Center for the First-Year Experience and Students in Transition at the University of South Carolina. Her work centers on providing educators with resources to develop personal and professional skills while creating and refining innovative programs designed to increase undergraduate student learning and success.*

NEW DIRECTIONS FOR STUDENT SERVICES • DOI: 10.1002/ss

2

Understanding the prime-time television portrait of college helps educators better understand the expectations our entering students may hold of college life.

Beyond Demographics: Understanding the College Experience Through Television

Barbara F. Tobolowsky

For decades, educators have recognized that students' background characteristics affect their college-going experiences. Therefore, surveys ask about demographic information, socioeconomic status, and parental educational backgrounds, knowing that these variables influence a student's college life. However, these characteristics do not tell the whole story. Exposure to popular media also influences student expectations (Tobolowsky, 2001), and expectations affect students' adjustment to college (Gerdes and Mallinckrodt, 1994), their satisfaction with their institution, and their persistence to graduation (Braxton, Vesper, and Hossler, 1995; Tinto, 1993). These images contribute to deep-seated, and often unexamined, perceptions of the college experience.

It is important to understand the popular image of college represented in the media because it can have a powerful impact on a student's ultimate success at an institution. To gain a more holistic view of our incoming students so that we can be truly prepared to address their needs, this chapter explores the following aspects of the prime-time portrait: televisual colleges and the importance of college attendance, the intellectual as comic fodder, first-year student adjustment, faculty and staff (non)support, and academic challenges such as grades and the trauma of finals.

New Directions for Student Services, no. 114, Summer 2006 © Wiley Periodicals, Inc.
Published online in Wiley InterScience (www.interscience.wiley.com) • DOI: 10.1002/ss.204

17

Prime-Time College

Television has been depicting the college experience since the 1950s. In the late 1990s and early 2000s, the number of television series set on fictional campuses grew to approximately ten series that depicted college life. Most of these series were told from the student perspective. Significantly, the series that focused on student characters were intended to appeal to younger audiences. Since a number of media studies suggest a link between televisual images and perceptions held by viewers (Palmer, Smith, and Strawser, 1993; Signorielli, 1993; Weimann, 2000; Williams, 1986), it is likely those series appealing to younger viewers may help shape their expectations of college. Thus, it is to those series we turn our attention.

The discussion that follows is based on episodes from the following series, all of which focus on the first-year college experience of their main characters: *Boy Meets World* (1998–1999 season), *Felicity* (1998–1999), *Sabrina, the Teenage Witch* (2000–2001), *Buffy the Vampire Slayer* (1999–2000), *Moesha* (1999–2000), *The Parkers* (1999–2000), and *7th Heaven* (2000–2001). A brief description of the main characters in each series is presented in Exhibit 2.1.

Before detailing the specific elements of the televisual portrait of college, it is worth noting a few general observations. First, from the premiere episodes, college played a central role on only two of the series, *Felicity* and *The Parkers*. The entire first season of *Felicity* is about her first-year college experience. Similarly, the central element of *The Parkers* is that Kim Parker, eighteen years old, and her mother, Nikki, thirty-six years old, enter Santa Monica College together as first-year students. The key concept of this series is how a mother and daughter deal with the college experience from their very different places in life.

In contrast, four of the series started with their characters in high school (*Buffy*, *7th Heaven*, *Moesha*, and *Sabrina*) or middle school (*Boy Meets*

Exhibit 2.1. Main Characters of Television Series Referred to in This Chapter.

Boy Meets World: A group of predominantly white students from middle school through college.

Buffy: The Vampire Slayer: A young woman who battles demons while dealing with the normal problems of a teenager.

Felicity: A young, naïve girl who goes to college in New York.

Moesha: An African American young woman during her high school and college years in California.

The Parkers: An African American mother and daughter who attend the same California community college (a spin-off of *Moesha*).

Sabrina: The Teenage Witch: A young witch learning about her powers from her two witch aunts during her high school and college years.

7th Heaven: A minister, his wife, and their seven children, many of whom attend college.

NEW DIRECTIONS FOR STUDENT SERVICES • DOI: 10.1002/ss

World) when the series premiered. Over the course of their television run, the characters graduated from high school and continued on to college. This is significant because it was the long-standing success of the shows that necessitated the characters graduate from high school, and the creators decided to send them to college.

In only two series does a character choose not to go to college after high school, and each series explores that decision. In *7th Heaven,* Mary Camden's decision not to go to college was grist for a well-developed story line about the problems and disappointments associated with her choice.

In *Buffy the Vampire Slayer,* Xander's choice not to attend college leaves him feeling distanced from his now college-going former high school friends. In one episode, thinking a magic spell has left his friends unable to see or hear him, Xander expresses his frustration with the comment, "Not that the-didn't-go-to-college guy has anything important to say."

Xander and Mary's experiences are rare in prime-time. In fact, college is the natural life choice for most prime-time characters (McDonough, 1997; Terenzini and others, 1994). Statistically, only 40 percent of high school graduates enroll immediately in college (Achieve, Inc., 2006; McDonough, 1997; Terenzini and others, 1994). Therefore, the college-going pattern on prime-time is not the same as what is in evidence nationally.

The Intellectual as Comic Fodder

College may be the next step after high school for fictional teens, but academic pursuits are primary sources of humor on episodic television. In *Sabrina,* the intellectual enthusiasm of Miles, Sabrina's roommate, and Zelda, a professor and Sabrina's aunt, are often presented as comical. Miles, who has no romantic or social connections, speaks passionately about physics. Zelda, a professor, can relate to his academic excitement as well as his experience of "people's eyes glazing over" when he speaks of his passion. The audience (as evidenced by the laugh track) finds humor in what could be perceived as these characters' misplaced emotions.

In one episode of *Moesha,* the title character tutors a star basketball player who tells her he had expected her to be a geek because he heard she was an advanced placement freshman. As with Miles, the message is that if you do well in school, you are expected to have little social currency.

Buffy represents the nonintellectual in *Buffy the Vampire Slayer.* She decides not to take "Introduction to the Modern Novel," for example, because she suspects she would have to read novels. In another episode, a teaching assistant notes a downturn in her work and mentions he has not seen her hand up in class in a long time. Buffy asks if stretching counts. Since she is the main character, Buffy's stance underscores an anti-intellectual attitude in the series. Buffy can do things the other characters cannot (for example, she can save the world from demons), but she has no interest in academic pursuits. In fact, Willow, the resident intellectual in *Buffy,* worries that people see her as a nerd because she is smart. So, the series implies, what good is being smart when it is not valued by the outside world?

First-Year Student Adjustment

First-year students have the highest level of distress of all student cohorts (Greene, 1998). This fact should come as no surprise, considering the extraordinary changes and challenges these highly successful young people must confront. One reason students may have serious adjustment issues is that they hold an unrealistic expectation of college. As Tinto (1993) states, "When [college] expectations are either unrealistic and/or seriously mistaken, subsequent experiences can lead to major disappointments" (p. 54). Many of the challenges and expectations that real first-year students face also find voice in prime-time television.

The most common expectation depicted by the television characters in the series under consideration is that college is a time of adjustment. For instance, as the time for Sabrina to attend college nears, Sabrina and her aunts reveal their differing expectations of the experience. Anticipating Sabrina's study needs, her aunt Zelda magically changes her room into an ornate Elizabethan study, with large bookcases and a desk. Hilda, her other aunt and a graduate of clown school, has a different concept of college and magically decorates Sabrina's room with bright colors, stuffed clowns, and balloons, suggesting college is a time of fun. Sabrina agrees that college is a time of change, but her focus is not on her bedroom décor. Rather, she wants to live in campus housing "like a normal freshman." She sees herself as "embarking on a journey of independent self-discovery," and expects that college will offer her a chance to claim her independence.

The expectation that college is a time to stretch oneself and try new things can be coupled with a tinge of anxiety in these series. For instance, Buffy looks for reassurance from her friend Willow when she says, "college is a time of change, right?" Willow agrees, "What's college for if not experimenting?" Although Willow and Buffy attend a college only five miles from their homes, Willow talks excitedly about entering "uncharted territory." She expects it to be a "place of energy where your mind opens up and lets this place spurt knowledge" into it. Later in that episode about her first day on campus, Buffy appears overwhelmed. As she walks through the crowded plaza, she is exhorted to protest against the campus administration, watches while fraternity pledges in their underwear snake through the crowd, is asked if she accepts Jesus, and is invited to do Jell-O shots at a fraternity party. Eventually, she finds her friend, Willow, and confesses that this first taste of college is "almost too much."

The series offers numerous other examples of Buffy's difficult college transition. She continually reminds herself that there are many adjustments as she encounters different obstacles, such as getting lost on campus, getting used to her roommate, and dealing with academic demands. At one point another student consoles her by saying that "it [college] is supposed to get easier." Within a few episodes, Buffy finds that forecast to come true. After winning a particularly tough battle with demons, she finally sighs with relief that college is not such a scary place after all. In fact, she declares, "It's just like high school," suggesting that she can handle whatever problems (or demons) come her way.

Felicity's adjustment to college is quite difficult as well. One reason, perhaps, is that she selected her school because a boy she was interested in at high school was going there. Very early on she has to face the reality that a relationship with him is unlikely. When she first encounters him there he is not only with another woman, but he doesn't remember her name. This is not the only time she is crushed in the episode. After each disappointment, Felicity appears shell-shocked. She says she "feels lost" and unable "to find solace in anything." She briefly considers returning home but rather than have to admit her error to her parents, she decides to stay at school even though she recognizes the road ahead will be difficult.

At various junctures, Felicity is told that this time, the beginning of her first year, is particularly difficult. Noel, the resident advisor, tells her that though things are heightened now, she just needs to give it a month and things will normalize. He tries to encourage her to keep things in perspective, telling her, "Just keep repeating, 'It's only college.'"

Adjustment is an issue in other series as well. After just the first day of college classes, Sabrina fears she is falling behind. Morgan, her resident advisor, tells her this is what "every freshman goes through" and advises Sabrina to "party, party, party." Sabrina reluctantly follows Morgan's recommendation and as a result her schoolwork suffers. Her Aunt Hilda points out that she will eventually learn how to balance her time, giving the message that one important part of the adjustment is balancing one's social life and academic responsibilities.

Beyond issues of balance, the series highlight the divide between life before college and life as a college student. One way this divide is illustrated is by comparing collegiate academic demands with students' high school experience. For example, Moesha, an A student in high school, is getting a C in college chemistry. She tells her father, "I've never studied this hard for any class and all I have to show for it is a C." He reminds her that college courses are more demanding. This idea is also depicted in *Boy Meets World* when the English professor comments on the students' poor essay papers by saying, "This isn't high school. Free up your minds. You're smarter than this."

Positive differences from high school are also noted. In *Felicity*, characters remark that they no longer have to worry about being tardy, getting a hall pass, or dealing with hall monitors. Willow and Buffy are surprised and excited by the range of courses available to them, from "Introduction to Popular Culture" to "Ethnomusicology."

Still, the change can be wrenching for some of the characters. Sabrina's aunts worry that she will no longer have time for them. Sometimes, the college student acutely feels the separation. For example, when Buffy returns home to recover from her college experiences, she finds that she no longer fits in there, literally and figuratively: her mom has turned her bedroom into a storage room.

In other instances, the student uses the distance from home as a way to avoid family issues. In *7th Heaven,* for example, Matt stays away from home to find respite from dealing with his troubled sister.

The difficulties associated with the first-year of college do not persist indefinitely for the characters. After a few episodes, Buffy feels able to handle any problems she will face, and Felicity eventually feels comfortable in her new environment. For the characters in the other series, their periods of adjustment are shown to be brief or not as challenging.

Faculty and Staff (Non)support

Since academic pursuits are often portrayed in a comical way and intellectual characters are subjected to mocking representations, how does the seemingly most educated person at the prime-time college, the professor, fare in these series? Educatonal research suggests that students felt faculty "took a personal interest" in them (Levine and Cureton, 1998, p. 130). Is this relationship reflected in prime-time?

In the majority of instances, the prime-time student does not have a nurturing, positive relationship with his or her professor. *Felicity* believes the renowned chemistry professor, Dr. Garabay, hates her, when he answers her questions brusquely and advises her, "If you want to be teacher's pet, sign up for Mr. Jurgeson's class. He's not tenured." Felicity says, "I don't have to be teacher's pet. I don't want to be teacher's pet." "Then you'll do just fine," answers Garabay. He continues, "The beauty is you don't have to be okay with me to learn something in my class. My advice is don't worry about me, worry about you."

This exchange brings up several interesting ideas. The first is that a tenured professor is less interested in the personal development of his students than the nontenured faculty person. Are the nontenured faculty more student-centered because of their more tenuous position? Second, this interaction shows that the differences between college and high school can be disorienting to the student. Although Felicity was an excellent student in high school, in this new setting she does not understand her professor's more distant attitude. She expects the professor to relate to students in terms of liking or disliking them. Here she is introduced to the notion that a student's job is to learn, and they should put aside personal feelings that get in the way of that goal. Is Garabay right? Do personal feelings have a place in the classroom? Do they have an impact on the ability of the student to learn and the professor to teach? For some prime-time students, like Felicity, understanding this different faculty role is part of their adjustment to becoming serious students.

NEW DIRECTIONS FOR STUDENT SERVICES • DOI: 10.1002/ss

The representation of faculty in *Felicity* is not an anomaly. Buffy encounters somewhat stereotypically gruff faculty in her first two classes at college: one tells her she is "wasting everyone's time" by interrupting his lecture and being in the room without being registered for the class. He tells her she is "sucking energy from everyone in the room" and orders her to leave. At her next class, the professor introduces her teaching methods rather sternly: "Make no mistake, I run a hard class. I assign a lot of work, talk fast, and expect you to keep up. If you are looking to cruise, you should take Geology 101. All the football players are there." In a later class with this teacher, Buffy is scolded for missing class (she had some slaying to do). "If you have problems," says this teacher, "you need to solve them on your own time. If you miss again, you're out."

Not all series depict professors as tough and unhelpful. *7th Heaven* offers a different perspective. Matt, who is not doing well in chemistry, shares with his professor some of the personal problems he's been going through. The professor at this point is unsympathetic. However, when later in the episode, Matt approaches the professor in the library and reluctantly asks for help, explaining he fears doing so is a sign of weakness, the professor says, "Asking for help isn't a sign of weakness, it's a sign of maturity." He reminds Matt that he promised he would help any student who asked and encourages Matt to come by his office for help.

This professor offers his own brand of tough love, but he also provides some needed support to Matt. As with the others, this series presents a different picture of a teacher-student relationship than what might be expected in high school. However, unlike some of the other student-faculty interactions depicted at these fictional colleges, this professor did help after the student put his best efforts into learning the material.

There is a similar example in *Moesha*. When Moesha has trouble understanding her chemistry class, the professor writes what appears to be a formula on the board in response to one of Moesha's questions. Moesha admits she does not understand that either. The professor decodes her scribbles as when and where she offers her office hours. Being such a strong student in high school, it is hard for Moesha to accept that she is having difficulty now. Moesha never goes to the professor. Rather, the narrative shows Moesha eventually getting help from a friend. Through these examples, we learn that prime-time professors do not provide the kind of sensitive handling students may want or need, but they do offer help.

In these series, learning is paramount and the idea of nurturing their students is not a priority for most of the prime-time professors. Still, the portrait does include some professors who offer assistance in ways that students may or may not feel comfortable accepting.

Curiously, rarely are other campus representatives depicted in these series. The sole exceptions are the rare glimpses of a college president in *Boy Meets World* and an academic advisor in *Felicity*. The president is brought in when there is a judicial hearing regarding improper student behavior in *Boy Meets World*. The advisor, however, has a reoccurring role in *Felicity*. This individual serves as sounding board, therapist, and friend to Felicity as she deals with issues with her parents, changing majors, breaking school rules, and academic honesty. Because television helps create expectations of the college experience in viewers, the lack of administrative staff represented in prime-time may explain why many people have a limited understanding of the range of administrative staff that function on our college campuses.

Grades

Closely linked to the representation of faculty are the students' concerns about grades. If faculty do not provide the kind of help prime-time students want, no wonder they worry about how they fare in their classrooms. This fear is not limited to television. As Greene (1998) contends, "The anxiety-producing factors that dominate the [real] campus environment—doing well and having future opportunities—create a conscious focus on grades" (p. 38). Several of the series reflect these concerns. In *Boy Meets World*, some characters worry more about grades than others. For instance, Angela is nervous to see what she got on her first college paper, but is happy when she gets a B+. Cory and Shawn are ecstatic when they get Bs. Even though Topanga, another student, congratulates Cory and Shawn on their Bs, she is livid when she finds out she also got one, revealing a level of competitiveness that drives many college students' feelings about their grades.

Grades often are seen in a comparative light, as in the *Boy Meets World* example. Topanga is unhappy with a B, whereas the grade is considered good for the guys. We have already discussed Moesha's concern over a C in her chemistry class and her father's effort to console her. Getting an average grade devastates Moesha and even more so because her friend, Neecy, got an A.

In *The Parkers*, one sycophant who is pledging a sorority with Kim at Santa Monica College says the "scaredest" she has ever been was when she thought she got a C in Chemistry. In contrast, Kim speaks proudly of her C average in a later episode.

The Trauma of Finals

The concern over grades is more intensely in evidence when the characters face final exams. In *Felicity*, an intense level of stress is associated with the importance of exams. Felicity says, "It [finals] was insane. . . . and I knew [that] for three days I would be in hell." Noel talks about how a family emergency kept him from studying for finals and now, "My educational future hangs in a balance." Such histrionics are common in the episode. Later on he rants, "I'm in the middle of finals, which threaten my very existence as a

NEW DIRECTIONS FOR STUDENT SERVICES • DOI: 10.1002/ss

student." Felicity comments on how stressed out everyone is and is told, "Yeah, it's finals." This response suggests that the intensity and anxiety are normal. In this episode, students pull all-nighters, study in groups, take drugs to stay awake, and live in the library for the three days of finals week.

A similarly high stress level is depicted in *Boy Meets World,* where Rachel, Jack, and Eric are too jumpy to study in their apartment, where every click of a pen or chomp of an apple sends them reeling. Because finals count for 90 percent of their grade, they are understandably tense. They head to the library, hoping to find a place more conducive to studying, but only find more stressed-out students screaming at each other while they attempt to study. Eric eventually yells at them to stop, telling them that "Finals are turning us into monsters." He admits that exams are "important to our futures, not just here at Pennbrook [their university], but for the rest of our lives." Finals are once again depicted as incredibly important, difficult, stress-inducing events.

Conclusion

What are the consistent and stable images associated with college, this all-encompassing aspect of the academic life of prime-time students? College is the natural step after high school for most prime-time students. They have limited expectations of the experience, but express notions of exercising independence for the first time as well as acknowledging it will be a time of change and adjustment. Once there, these students must attempt to adjust to a far different life from the one they led in high school. One major concern is stress and worry over grades.

Though grades and doing well are important, the life of the mind is often used as grist for the comedy mill. Intellectual pursuits are often depicted in a comedic manner. Professors are frequently presented as tough taskmasters, insensitive to their students' fragile egos. Since professors embody the notion of the intellectual, it is not surprising that their depiction is less than flattering. Also, the shows are depicted from the student perspective, so the faculty is a natural adversary for the students, providing conflict in the stories. Curiously, students are not shown having other campus advocates in most of these series. Therefore, the depiction of uncaring faculty suggests an equally unyielding institution. In prime-time, students must rely largely on themselves and their friends to make it through the first year.

These images may contribute to entering students' view of college. With such a limited picture, new students may not be sure where to turn as they meet difficulties along the way. By understanding how our students' expectations may be shaped by prime-time programming, we can be more aware of their concerns, proactive in our efforts, and provide necessary information that counters any unrealistic expectations based on media. Our job is to ensure that our students do not feel like Buffy or Felicity or Moesha in that crucial early period of adjustment.

References

Abrams, J. J., and Reeves, M. (creators) (1998–1999). *Felicity*. Los Angeles: WB.

Achieve, Inc. *Closing the Expectation Gap 2006*. Washington, D.C.: Achieve, Inc., 2006. http://www.achieve.org/dstore.nsf/Lookup/50-statepub-06.pdf.

Braxton, J. M., Vesper, N., and Hossler, D. "Expectations for College and Student Persistence." *Research in Higher Education*, 1995, *36*(5), 595–611.

Farquhar, R. R., Finney, S. V., and Spears, V. (creators) (1999–2000). *Moesha*. Los Angeles: UPN.

Finney, S. V., Spears, V., and Farquhar, R. R. (creators) (1999–2000). *The Parkers*. Los Angeles: UPN.

Gerdes, H. and Mallinckrodt, B. "Emotional, Social, and Academic Adjustment of College Students: A Longitudinal Study of Retention." *Journal of Counseling and Development*, Jan.-Feb. 1994, *72*, 281–288.

Greene, H. R. *The Select: Realities of Life and Learning in America's Elite Colleges*. New York: HarperCollins, 1998.

Hampton, B. (creator) (2000–2001). *7th Heaven*. Los Angeles: WB.

Jacobs, M., and Kelly, A. (creators) (1998–1999). *Boy Meets World*. Los Angeles: ABC.

Levine, A., and Cureton, J. S. *When Hope and Fear Collide: A Portrait of Today's College Student*. San Francisco: Jossey-Bass, 1998.

McDonough, P. M. *Choosing Colleges: How Social Class and Schools Structure Opportunity*. Albany, N.Y.: State University of New York Press, 1997.

Palmer, E. L., Smith, K. T., and Strawser, K. S. "Rubik's Tube: Developing Child's Television Worldview." In G. L. Berry and J. K. Asamen (eds.), *Children and Television: Images in a Changing Socio-Cultural World*. Thousand Oaks, Calif.: Sage, 1993.

Prestwich, D., Yorkin, N., and Holcomb, R. (exec. producers) (2001–2002). *The Education of Max Bickford*. Los Angeles: CBS.

Schmock, J. (developer) (2000–2001). *Sabrina, the Teenage Witch*. Based on characters appearing in *Archie* Comics. Los Angeles: WB.

Signorielli, N. "Television, the Portrayal of Women, and Children's Attitudes." In G. L. Berry and J. K. Asamen (eds.), *Children and Television: Images in a Changing Socio-Cultural World*. Thousand Oaks, Calif.: Sage, 1993.

Terenzini, P. T., and others. "The Transition to College: Diverse Students, Diverse Stories." *Research in Higher Education*, 1994, *35*(1), 57–73.

Tinto, V. *Leaving Colleges: Rethinking the Causes and Cures of Student Attrition*. (2nd ed.) Chicago: University of Chicago Press, 1993.

Tobolowsky, B. F. "The Influence of Prime-Time Television on Latinas' College Aspirations and Expectations." Unpublished doctoral dissertation, Department of Education and Information Studies, University of California Los Angeles, 2001.

Weimann, G. *Communicating Unreality: Modern Media and the Reconstruction of Reality*. Thousand Oaks, Calif.: Sage, 2000.

Whedon, J. (creator) (1999–2000). *Buffy the Vampire Slayer*. Los Angeles: WB.

Williams, T. M. *The Impact of Television: A Natural Experiment in Three Communities*. Orlando, Fla.: Academic Press, 1986.

BARBARA F. TOBOLOWSKY *is associate director of the National Resource Center for the First-Year Experience and Students in Transition at the University of South Carolina, where she is responsible for the Center's research and publication efforts.*

NEW DIRECTIONS FOR STUDENT SERVICES • DOI: 10.1002/ss

3

This chapter presents findings from a national research study with a sample of nearly twenty thousand first-year students on how students' experiences and campus programs affect key academic outcomes of the first year.

Promoting New-Student Success: Assessing Academic Development and Achievement Among First-Year Students

Jennifer R. Keup

College professors and professionals have long debated the purpose of higher education, its desired impact on students, and how such outcomes should be measured. At different times throughout history, the desired outcome of a college education focused on different aspects of the students themselves and society at large. For example, in the colonial era (1636–1789), the aim of higher education was the continuation of high culture in the upper classes of a fledgling American society. Later, during the university transformation era (1870–1944), vocational training for the changing American economy was the primary emphasis of postsecondary schooling. In the contemporary era (1976–present), we have again had to shift our focus to understanding how to consume and master information (that is, learning how to learn) in order to function in a rapidly changing society (Cohen, 1998; Goodchild and Wechsler, 1997; Lucas, 1994). However, at the core of any set of intended goals of higher education is the idea that the college experience educates students and imbues them with a set of intellectual and personal skills to be successful individuals in society. In other words, while we need to recognize the development that occurs among college students both cognitively and affectively (Astin, 1985; Bowen, 1977), one of the most pressing missions of higher education and a critical measure

NEW DIRECTIONS FOR STUDENT SERVICES, no. 114, Summer 2006 © Wiley Periodicals, Inc.
Published online in Wiley InterScience (www.interscience.wiley.com) • DOI: 10.1002/ss.205

of student success is developing academic and intellectual competence among our students.

Given this widely accepted aim of higher education, a large body of literature exists on the forces and factors contributing to students' academic success and achievement (as catalogued in Astin, 1993; Feldman and Newcomb, 1969; Kuh, Schuh, Whitt, and Associates, 1991; and Pascarella and Terenzini, 1991, 2005). However, very little of this work focuses exclusively on the first year of college, when students face challenges unique to the transition from high school to college, create habits and practices that are often sustained throughout college, and forge the foundation for the rest of their academic career (Erickson and Strommer, 1991; Schilling and Schilling, 1999, 2005; Upcraft, Gardner, and Associates, 1989). Further, several factors, including increased selectivity in higher education and competition for admission, have led to inflation of high school grades and very high student expectations for success in college, in spite of the fact that national statistics show that students are entering college with lower levels of academic preparation than in previous decades (Erickson and Strommer, 1991) as well as a history of significant academic disengagement in high school (Astin, Oseguera, Sax, and Korn, 2002). As such, first-year students often are ill-equipped for the academic demands of college during the first year, which may help explain declines in first-year collegiate achievement as measured by GPA, academic involvement, feelings of dissatisfaction, and low levels of interaction with faculty (Keup and Stolzenberg, 2004).

Student development theory also feeds the necessity for additional research on the academic development and achievement of first-year college students. Perry's theory of intellectual and ethical development and the host of cognitive structural theories that it spawned, including Kitchner and King's Reflective Judgment Model, Gilligan's Different Voice Model, and Baxter Magolda's Model of Epistemological Reflection (all summarized in Evans, Forney, and Guido-DiBrito, 1998; Kurfiss, 1988; Pascarella and Terenzini, 1991, 2005; and Upcraft, Gardner, and Associates, 1989), all identify a path of intellectual development for adolescents in general and college students in particular. These models generally represent intellectual and cognitive development as a journey from a dualistic, nonanalytical, passive mode of thinking through several stages to a final intellectual position in which students recognize knowledge and learning as contextual, evolutionary, and integrative, thereby requiring analysis and critical thinking. While theorists are not prescriptive about the timeline for development through these stages, research has indicated that traditional-aged entering college students tend to experience the first critical transition from the first to second stages during the first year of college, which then serves as the foundation of future cognitive-intellectual gains (Baxter Magolda, 1992; Erickson and Strommer, 1991; Kurfiss, 1988; Perry, 1981). It is therefore critical that higher education researchers and practitioners identify and leverage the practices and programs that can facilitate this critical stage of development among the entering student population and foster academic achievement during the first year and beyond.

One of the challenges of assessment in higher education is to determine how to measure academic gains in our students over time. While national surveys of the college student experience have proliferated over the years, assessment tools focusing specifically on the first-year experience have emerged only recently, thereby providing new data sources to address students' academic experiences, development, and achievement during the first year of college. One such survey, Your First College Year (YFCY), was designed as a one-year follow-up instrument to the Cooperative Institutional Research Program's (CIRP) annual Freshman Survey to assess the academic and personal development of students over the first year of college at numerous institutions across the country. The CIRP Freshman Survey and YFCY serve as the data source for the current research, thereby providing a comprehensive picture of first-year college experiences and the academic and intellectual development of students during this critical period of adjustment. The purpose of the current research is to use these data to provide a national perspective on how student experiences and campus programs affect academic and cognitive outcomes of the first year of college. Research of this nature allows higher education practitioners and decision makers to assess the effectiveness of their programs, pedagogies, and policies designed for first-year students and to add to the national dialogue on the topic of first-year student success.

Methodology

The study methodology is described in terms of data source and sample, variables, and analytical methods.

Data Source and Sample. The data used in this study represent a multi-institution sample drawn from the national population of first-time, full-time students at four-year colleges and universities across the country. This sample includes 19,995 students at 115 baccalaureate-granting colleges and universities who completed both the Cooperative Institutional Research Program's (CIRP) 2002 Freshman Survey, administered at college entry, and the 2003 Your First College Year (YFCY) survey, administered at the end of the students' first year.

As shown in Table 3.1, students attending public and private four-year institutions of all types, sizes, and selectivity levels were represented in this sample. Table 3.1 also outlines the important demographic characteristics of the sample, including the gender breakdown and the distribution of race or ethnicity, high school academic achievement, family income, and distance of the college from home. The combination of these two surveys provides a longitudinal database for a national cohort of students at four-year institutions across the country for whom we have data at the beginning and end of their first college year, allowing us to investigate various aspects of students' affective and cognitive development during the first year of college.

NEW DIRECTIONS FOR STUDENT SERVICES • DOI: 10.1002/ss

Table 3.1. Chracteristics of the CIRP-YFCY Longitudinal Sample.

Variable	Percent of Sample	Variable	Percent of Sample
Gender			
Men	36.7	High School GPA	
Women	63.3	A(A+)	28.9
		B+, A–	46.3
Race/Ethnicity*		B	16.7
White	82.7	B–, C+	7.2
Black	5.1	C or less	1.0
American Indian	1.5		
Asian	7.4		
Native Hawaiian	0.9	Parental Income	
Mexican American	2.8	< $20,000	6.3
Puerto Rican	1.0	$20,000–49,999	20.6
Other Latino	2.1	$50,000–99,999	40.4
Other	2.9	$100,000+	32.8
Institutional Type			
Public universities	18.4	Miles from College to Home	
Private universities	7.6	50 or less	25.7
Four-year colleges		51–100	19.4
Public	22.7	101–500	39.6
Nonsectarian	18.4	More than 500	15.3
Catholic	18.8		
Other religious	14.2		

Notes: N = 19,995. *Percentages will add to more than 100 since students were allowed to mark more than one category.

Analytical Methods. The longitudinal data comprised of first-year students' responses to the 2002 CIRP Freshman Survey and the 2003 YFCY were used in descriptive analyses to identify the nature of students' academic experiences during the first year. Further, multivariate analyses were conducted to provide a clearer understanding of the relationships between specific college experiences and key academic outcomes of the first year of college. To investigate and identify these potential relationships, this study employed a conceptual framework used in previous studies of college impact with CIRP data: Astin's Input-Environment-Outcome (I-E-O) model (1991), shown in Figure 3.1. This methodological framework attempts to adjust for the non-random assignment of people to particular environments in non-experimental studies of individuals. In other words, characteristics that students possess prior to attending college ("inputs") can, and do, simultaneously affect students' selection of particular institutional environments and their experiences in those settings as well as the "outcomes" of those particular environments.

In order to isolate the true impact of aspects of the college environment on student outcomes, input characteristics must first be considered and con-

Figure 3.1. Astin's I-E-O Model (1991).

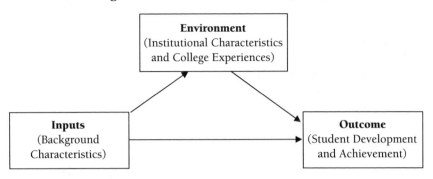

trolled. In doing so, we minimize the risk that the outcomes of college might be attributed falsely to the impact of the college experience when, in fact, they might merely reflect differences in students' personal experiences and background that were present prior to college entry (Astin, 1991).

In addition to controlling for students' personal lives and experiences prior to college, it is critical to consider the fact that participation in certain campus activities or experiences may be confounded with particular environmental characteristics. For example, certain institutional settings tend to offer more opportunities for campus involvement, a better student-to-faculty ratio, a culture of participation in student organizations, or superior student facilities, or to have more programs to ease the transition to college. To best assess the impact of various college experiences on student outcomes, it is critical that our analyses account for these biases.

The I-E-O model was used to guide our investigation of these data using blocked, stepwise regression analyses to identify the significant predictors of students' academic development during the first college year. In this method of multivariate data analysis, temporally ordered blocks of independent variables are allowed to enter the regression equation until no additional variables within a given block will produce a significant reduction of the residual sum of squares of the dependent variable. At this point, the variables in the next temporal block are considered for entry to help explain additional variance in the outcome measure (Astin, 1991; Pedhazur, 1997).

Variables. An initial factor analysis of the 2003 YFCY data yielded several factors that were used as variables in the regression analyses. One of these factors represents a dependent variable for the current study: students' self-assessed cognitive development. Measures of self-reported gains in four areas—analytical and problem-solving skills, critical thinking skills, general knowledge, and knowledge of a particular field or discipline—comprise this highly reliable factor (Cronbach's *alpha* = .79) and represent several of the skills that many theorists identify as necessary for advancement through the stages of intellectual development. Response options for these self-rated change items were on a five-point scale: "much weaker," "weaker," "no change," "stronger," and "much stronger."

Students' self-reported grade-point average from the first year, which was measured on a six-point scale ranging from A to C– or less, served as the other dependent variable. Given that academic grades are often the most tangible form of feedback that institutions provide to their students, this outcome represents a key measure of student achievement in college.

Independent variables for the study were organized into three temporally ordered blocks. Drawing from the I-E-O model, the first block contains input characteristics. Specifically, block one was comprised of demographic variables (gender and race or ethnicity) and socioeconomic status (family income and highest level of parental education). In addition, this block controlled for measures of academic achievement and self-confidence prior to college, including students' expectations that they would need extra time to earn their degree, high school grades (the pretest for first-year grade-point average), and five measures of students' academic self-concept prior to entering college. These five variables represented survey respondents' self-assessment of their ability in comparison to their peers on academic ability, drive to achieve, mathematical ability, intellectual self-confidence, and writing ability. In the absence of a direct pretest, these measures served as proxy pretests for the outcome measure of self-assessed cognitive development. By controlling for background characteristics that have profound effects on first-year students' behavior, college experiences, perceptions of their environment, self-concept, and achievement in earlier blocks, the researcher was better able to evaluate the true impact of college experiences on the academic and cognitive development of students over the first year of college.

Environmental variables were divided into two different blocks. First, eight important institutional controls were allowed to enter the regressions to account for the potentially biasing effects of various institutional types (that is, public universities, private universities, public four-year colleges, private nonsectarian four-year colleges, Catholic four-year colleges, and other religious four-year colleges), first-year living arrangement (on-campus versus off-campus residence), and distance of the college from home. The next block of environmental variables contained the primary independent variables of interest for this study—thirty-seven items representing first-year academic experiences and campus involvement. These included measures of students' time allocation, interaction with faculty and peers, campus involvement (for example, volunteerism and service work, participation in student clubs and groups, student employment), social or personal adjustment (a five-item factor), barriers to academic involvement (for example, employment, family responsibilities, social commitments), measures of academic engagement, a factor representing academic disengagement, and two factors representing satisfaction with academic facilities and academic experiences.

Missing data were replaced via the calculation of EM algorithms for all independent variables. Tolerance statistics were at acceptable levels to address issues of multicolinearity among the independent variables.

Results

Results of the study are described in terms of descriptive statistics and regression analyses.

Descriptive Statistics. While it does not provide a comprehensive list of independent variables included in the current study, Table 3.2 summarizes the results of frequency distributions on first-year academic experience and involvement measures.

In Table 3.2, we see, for example, that students generally are satisfied with their first-year academic experiences, facilities, and services. More than 80 percent of the sample indicated that they were "satisfied" or "very satisfied" with campus library facilities and services and approximately three-quarters of the survey respondents were similarly satisfied with classroom facilities and overall quality of instruction. Conversely, just over 60 percent rated their first-year experiences with academic advising as at least satisfying; fewer than half of the respondents were satisfied with the relevance of their coursework to their daily lives.

These data also indicate just over half of the sample reporting that they received tutoring during the first year, although it is important to note that most of these students reported using these services only "rarely." In addition, while more than 40 percent of these students reported that they took a first-year seminar, far fewer took advantage of honors courses, learning communities, and developmental coursework. It appears that, although these various curricular innovations and interventions are gaining a foothold in American higher education, only a minority of first-year students are taking part in these courses (Keup and Stolzenberg, 2004).

Students do appear to be engaging in collaborative practices with their peers with respect to their academics. The majority of survey respondents studied with other students and discussed course content with other students outside of class on a frequent or occasional basis during the first year of college. Further, more than 75 percent of first-year students in the sample felt empowered enough to speak up in class at least occasionally. However, students reported only moderate levels of interaction with faculty during office hours and low levels of interaction with academic advisors, counselors, and professors outside of class and office hours, thereby underutilizing these critical academic resources during the first year.

These data also yield some important indicators of academic disengagement among these first-year students. We see that 80 percent of these full-time students (that is, those typically carrying twelve to fifteen units) attend classes or labs eleven or more hours per week, but only one-third spent similar amounts of time studying or doing homework outside of

NEW DIRECTIONS FOR STUDENT SERVICES • DOI: 10.1002/ss

Table 3.2. Academic Activities During the First Year of College.

	Percent
Felt "Very satisfied" or "Satisfied" with:	
Library facilities and services*	80.5
Classroom facilities*	78.0
Overall quality of instruction*	74.8
Amount of contact with faculty	66.3
Relevance of coursework to future career plans	64.1
Tutoring or other academic assistance*	63.0
Academic advising*	60.9
Relevance of coursework to everyday life	49.3
Attended classes/labs 11 or more hours per week	79.5
Studied or did homework 11 or more hours per week	33.4
Received tutoring	50.5
Took a first-year adjustment course	43.7
Enrolled in honors course	12.5
Enrolled in learning communities	10.2
Enrolled in remedial/developmental courses	4.8
"Frequently"	
Used the Internet for research or homework	83.3
Felt bored in class	43.4
Felt that your courses inspired you to think in new ways	22.9
"Frequently" or "Occasionally"	
Studied with other students	90.7
Discussed courses with other students	87.7
Spoke up in class	76.4
Came late to class	64.9
Felt that your social life interfered with your schoolwork	49.4
Turned in "subpar" assignments	41.7
Skipped class	34.9
Felt intimidated by your professors	28.3
Felt that job responsibilities interfered with your schoolwork	22.1
Felt that family responsibilities interfered with your schoolwork	16.5
Worked with professor on research project	13.2
Interacted with the following at least monthly:	
Faculty during office hours	52.4
Faculty outside of class or office hours	38.6
Academic advisors or counselors	28.3

Notes: N = 19,995. *Percentages are calculated only for those students who reported access to or experience with each facility or service on their campus.

class. In addition, more than 40 percent of the sample reported that they "frequently" felt bored in class, which may help explain the fact that nearly two-thirds of these students came late to class at least "occasionally" and just over one-third of the sample reported that they skipped class "frequently" or "occasionally" during the first year. These data also show that more than 40 percent of these respondents "frequently" or "occasionally" turned in course assignments that they feel did not reflect their best work, and only 23 percent felt that their courses inspired them to think in new ways. This high degree of academic disengagement may be partially explained by the fact that first-year students appear to be balancing multiple commitments during their first year in college (for example, social lives, job responsibilities, and family obligations), which may interfere with their schoolwork.

Regression Analyses. Although descriptive analyses provide valuable information on the experiences of first-year students, multivariate analyses yield the maximum information about the potential causal connections among variables. Specifically, these multivariate analyses address the question of how the academic activities and measures of involvement highlighted in the descriptive analyses affect first-year grades and self-assessed cognitive development. Although personal and background characteristics are important to students' academic and personal growth in college, the following discussion of the findings for each outcome focuses primarily on the impact of first-year experiences and involvement measures. Further, our most effective means of enhancing the outcomes of college as higher education researchers, practitioners, and policymakers is through the experiences that students have in the academic setting.

Given their critical role in college admissions, first-to-second year retention, and as a measure of overall adjustment and achievement during the first year of college, undergraduates' grade-point average (GPA) represents an important outcome. These data show that students' grades generally decline slightly between high school and the first year of college, from approximately A– to a B average. The first multivariate analysis helps identify the college experiences that potentially explain this decrease in students' GPA. As shown in Table 3.3, seventeen control variables enter the regression equation prior to the block of college experiences. The input variable that has the largest effect on first-year college grades is the pretest—high school grades—followed by the student's rating of his or her own academic ability at college entry.

Once we account for the effects of background and institutional characteristics, twenty-nine college experience variables prove to have a statistically significant impact on students' grades during the first year of college. However, many of these variables do not have very high regression coefficients and do not cause a large increase in the explanation of variance of the dependent variable (R^2). While other college experiences have important negative consequences for the academic performance of first-year college students, such as receiving tutoring (a possible indicator of academic difficulties), feeling overwhelmed by all they had to do, and feeling intimidated by college professors, the most potent predictor of the decline in grades is academic disengagement. Given that the descriptive analyses indicate that these behaviors are rampant among this first-year cohort as measured by

NEW DIRECTIONS FOR STUDENT SERVICES • DOI: 10.1002/ss

Table 3.3. Variables Predicting College Grade-Point Average

			Beta after:		
Step Variable	R^2	r	Block 1	Block 2	Block 3
Block 1: Demographics and Background Characteristics					
1 Average grade in high school	.18	.42	.29***	.31***	.24***
2 Self-rated: Academic ability	.19	.33	.14***	.15***	.11***
3 Sex: Female	.20	.12	.09***	.09***	.07***
4 Race: White/Caucasian	.21	.12	.05***	.04***	.02***
5 Parents' education	.22	.12	.05***	.05***	.04***
6 Self-rated: Drive to achive	.22	.20	.06***	.06***	.03***
7 Expectation: Need extra time for degree	.22	.15	.05***	.05***	.03***
8 Race: African American/Black	.22	-.13	-.05***	-.06***	-.06***
9 Self-rated: Writing ability	.22	.16	.04***	.04***	.02*
10 Race: Mexican American/Chicano	.23	-.07	-.04***	-.04***	-.03***
11 Parental income	.23	.09	.03***	.03***	.02**
12 Race: Native Hawaiian/Pacific Islander	.23	-.03	-.02**	-.02**	-.01
13 Self-rated: Intellectual self-confidence	.23	.10	-.02**	-.02*	-.03***
Block 2: Institutional Characteristics					
14 Public university	.23	.00	-.08***	-.09***	-.04***
15 Four-year public college	.23	-.07	-.02***	-.04***	-.01*
16 Lived on campus	.24	.01	-.03***	-.03***	-.03***
17 "Other" religious four-year college	.24	.01	.04***	.02*	.02*
Block 3: First-Year Experience and Involvement					
18 Academic Disengagement Factor	.27	-.28	-.19***	-.19***	-.16***
19 Enrolled in an honors course	.28	.23	.12***	.12***	.09***

20 Academic Satisfaction Factor	.29	.19	.14***	.13***	.10***
21 Frequency: Received tutoring	.30	-.16	-.11***	-.11***	-.11***
22 Frequency: Spoke up in class	.31	.15	.11***	.10***	.07***
23 Poor Social and Emotional Adjustment Factor	.31	.05	.01	.02*	.09***
24 Frequency: Felt overwhelmed	.31	-.07	-.10***	-.10***	-.06***
25 Hours per week: Participating in student clubs/groups	.32	.10	.04***	.04***	.04***
26 Frequency: Intimidated by your professors	.32	-.06	-.10***	-.09***	-.06***
27 Frequency: Courses inspired you to think in new ways	.32	.16	.10***	.10***	.04***
28 Frequency: Family duties interfered with your schoolwork	.32	-.09	-.06***	-.07***	-.03***
29 Hours per week: Studying/doing homework	.33	.19	.07***	.07***	.03***
30 Hours per week: Socializing with friends	.33	-.07	-.06***	-.06***	-.03***
31 Satisfaction: Tutoring/other academic assistance	.33	.06	.05***	.04***	.06***
32 Satisfaction with Academic Facilities Factor	.33	.04	.01	.00	-.05***
33 Frequency: Discussed course content with students outside of class	.33	.13	.05***	.05***	.03***
34 Took a first-year seminar	.33	.03	.05***	.04***	.03***
35 Interacted with academic advisors/counselors	.33	-.04	.00	-.01*	-.02***
36 Frequency: Felt bored in class	.33	-.08	-.07***	-.06***	.03***
37 Hours per week: Working (for pay) on campus	.33	.03	.03**	.02**	.02***
38 Financial concerns	.33	-.07	-.04***	-.05***	-.02***
39 Satisfaction: Academic advising	.33	.02	.02**	.02*	-.02***
40 Frequency: Drank alcohol	.33	-.12	-.08***	-.08***	-.02**
41 Hours per week: Attending classes/labs	.33	.13	.05***	.05***	.02**
42 Frequency: Studied with other students	.33	.00	-.03***	-.03***	-.02***
43 Enrolled in a remedial/developmental course	.33	-.08	-.03***	-.02***	-.02**
44 Frequency: Participated in volunteer/community service work	.33	.10	.04***	.03***	.02**
45 Frequency: Worked with professor on a research project	.33	-.03	.02*	.00	.01*
46 Frequency: Used the Internet for research or homework	.33	.05	.02**	.02**	.01*

*Notes: N = 19,572. *p < .05; **p < .01; ***p < .001.*

class attendance patterns, time spent on studying and coursework, and quality of first-year assignments, the somewhat predictable negative impact on first-year grades is quite concerning and an important reminder to faculty and academic administrators and staff who work with first-year students to find avenues to engage these students intellectually.

Despite the overall decline in grades, several college activities worked to facilitate academic performance in college. As one might predict, these measures represent academic involvement: enrolling in an honors course, satisfaction with academic aspects of college (that is, overall quality of instruction, relevance of coursework to everyday life, relevance of coursework to future career plans, and amount of contact with faculty), speaking up in class, and satisfaction with tutoring and other academic assistance. Since this last measure had the opposite impact on the outcome than the frequency of receiving tutoring, it is important to note that the quality of the tutorial experience is just as important as the quantity and a far more positive indicator of academic achievement as measured by grades. Interestingly, poor social and emotional adjustment (a factor comprised of feeling worried about meeting people, lonely or homesick, isolated from campus life, worried about health, and depressed) has a modest positive relationship with first-year grades. Since socializing with friends had a slight negative influence on the outcome variable and time spent studying or doing homework had a small positive impact on first-year GPA, it is possible that first-year students who had difficulty adjusting socially may have had more time to dedicate to their studies and, therefore, achieved higher grades in the midst of their struggles to feel connected to the campus community.

Although the feedback provided on a student's transcript is important, it does not encompass all aspects of academic achievement. Students' own perception of their gains in various intellectual areas also speaks to their academic and cognitive development. It is important, then, to evaluate the impact of college experiences on other measures of academic achievement and intellectual development, such as students' own feelings of their gains in cognitive abilities during the first year, including analytical and problem-solving skills, critical-thinking skills, general knowledge, and knowledge of a specific field or discipline. Similar to the regression for first-year GPA, Table 3.4 shows that several control variables enter the regression equation, including ten demographic and background measures and three institutional characteristics.

Although several of the self-rated measures of skills and abilities enter the equation, the one that has the highest simple correlation and proves to be the strongest predictor of the outcome from block one is the self-rated "drive to achieve" at college entry. The other self-rated abilities that enter the equation, although they do not add greatly to the explanation of variance, reflect students' feelings about their academic ability, intellectual self-confidence, and writing ability at college entry.

After the control variables were allowed to enter the regression, nineteen variables from the block of first-year experience and involvement measures were part of the final model. The variables that have the highest simple correlation and, similarly, prove to be the strongest predictors of self-assessed cognitive development are satisfaction with academic experiences (overall quality of instruction, relevance of coursework to everyday life, relevance of coursework to future career, amount of contact with faculty) and the frequency with which first-year students' courses inspired them to think in new ways. It is interesting to note that the language used on the items contained within these two measures reflects the issue of personal meaning and discovery in first-year coursework (for example, "inspired" and "relevance"). Although the items that were most significant to the previous regression seemed to require more involvement from the students, the two measures that are most significant to self-rated cognitive development represent more of a call to arms for institutional personnel with respect to course content and delivery.

Several other variables had relatively high correlations with the dependent variable; however, they shared enough variance with these two measures that only three other independent variables remained statistically significant to the final step, with a *beta* coefficient of .05 or greater. All three of these survey items are positive predictors of the outcome and the two strongest—hours per week spent studying or doing homework and discussing course content with students outside of class—represent important measures of time spent on college coursework.

While it is interesting to identify what is significant to each dependent variable respectively, it is also interesting to look across the two regression equations. For example, the nineteen first-year experience and involvement variables that predicted self-assessed cognitive development represent a subset of those that entered the analysis for first-year GPA. As such, one might assume that the objective of facilitating students' perceptions of their cognitive development would be met automatically by focusing on enhancing the factors that foster higher first-year grades. While this may be true, the fact that only one measure—the academic satisfaction factor—is statistically significant to the last step of both regression equations and had a *beta* coefficient of at least .05 suggests that this may not be the most effective means of promoting students' ratings of their change in their cognitive abilities. In other words, although enhancing students' feelings of satisfaction with the overall quality of instruction, amount of contact with faculty, and relevance of their coursework to their daily lives as well as to their career plans may be advantageous to both academic outcomes, there are specific aspects of the first-year experience that may prove particularly effective for one or the other aspect of student development (for example, focusing on lowering academic disengagement in order to yield higher first-year grades and an emphasis on offering coursework that inspires students to think in new ways to effect change on self-assessed cognitive development).

It is also important to note variables that have a different direction of effect on the respective outcomes in order to inform first-year programs and to understand fully the implications of campus practices. The most

NEW DIRECTIONS FOR STUDENT SERVICES • DOI: 10.1002/ss

Table 3.4. Variables Predicting Self-Assessed Cognitive Development.

Step Variable	R^2	r	Block 1	Beta after: Block 2	Block 3
Block 1: Demographics and Background Characteristics					
1 Self-rated: Drive to achive	.04	.19	.14***	.13***	.05***
2 Self-rated: Academic ability	.04	.13	.03***	.03***	.03***
3 Self-rated: Intellectual self-confidence	.04	.12	.04**	.04**	.01**
4 Average grade in high school	.04	.12	.06***	.06***	.02*
5 Self-rated: Writing ability	.05	.10	.04***	.04***	.01
6 Expectation: Need extra time for degree	.05	.08	.03***	.03***	.00
7 Race: Mexican American/Chicano	.05	.03	.02***	.03***	.01
8 Parental income	.05	.03	.03***	.02**	.00
9 Race: White/Caucasian	.05	-.03	-.03***	-.03***	-.05***
10 Sex: Female	.05	-.01	-.02*	-.02**	-.07***
Block 2: Institutional Characteristics					
11 Four-year public college	.05	-.08	-.06***	-.07***	.00
12 Public university	.05	.01	.02*	-.04***	.04***
13 Nonsectarian four-year college	.05	.05	.05***	.03***	.00

Block 3: First-Year Experience and Involvement

14 Academic Satisfaction Factor	.21	.42	.41***	.41***	.25***
15 Frequency: Courses inspired you to think in new ways	.26	.39	.37***	.37***	.22***
16 Hours per week: Studying/doing homework	.28	.23	.20***	.19***	.09***
17 Frequency: Discussed course content with students outside of class	.29	.24	.21***	.21***	.07***
18 Satisfaction with Academic Facilities Factor	.29	.23	.21***	.21***	.04***
19 Frequency: Used the Internet for research or homework	.29	.11	.10***	.10***	.05***
20 Frequency: Studied with other students	.29	.15	.14***	.14***	.03***
21 Frequency: Worked with professor on a research project	.30	.12	.12***	.12***	.04***
22 Satisfaction: Tutoring/other academic assistance	.30	.22	.20***	.20***	.02**
23 Hours per week: Attending classes/labs	.30	.11	.09***	.09***	.03***
24 Poor Social and Emotional Adjustment Factor	.30	-.07	-.06***	-.06***	-.03***
25 Frequency: Felt overwhelmed by all you had to do	.30	.01	.01	.01	.02***
26 Academic Disengagement Factor	.30	-.12	-.09***	-.08***	-.03***
27 Satisfaction: Academic advising	.30	.18	.17***	.17***	.02**
28 Frequency: Received tutoring	.30	.08	.08***	.09***	.02***
29 Frequency: Drank alcohol	.30	-.03	-.01	-.01	.02**
30 Frequency: Spoke up in class	.30	.18	.15***	.14***	.02**
31 Satisfaction: Orientation for new students	.30	.17	.16***	.16***	.02**
32 Hours per week: Participating in student clubs/groups	.30	.08	.04***	.04***	-.01*

Notes: $N = 19,605$. *$p < .05$; **$p < .01$; ***$p < .001$.

significant example for the current study is the differential impact of receiving tutoring. As mentioned earlier, engaging in tutoring has a negative relationship with grades, as evidenced by the simple correlation ($r = -.16$) and the regression coefficient in the final model for first-year GPA ($beta = -.11$) and may actually serve as a proxy for students in academic difficulty. However, although not among the most significant predictors at the final step of the regression for self-assessed cognitive development, receiving tutoring has a small, positive relationship with this outcome. Therefore, it would appear that the benefits from tutoring that manifest during the first year are less tangible than grades and speak to a broader issue of self-concept with respect to cognitive abilities. Although this result of the tutoring experience is meaningful in itself, it is important to note that many first-year students may seek tutoring because of lower academic performance and may not immediately recognize the more abstract notion of enhancement in cognitive skills. Therefore, faculty and academic advisors may want to help students set realistic expectations for GPA improvement when it comes to tutoring experiences during the first year (for example, informing them that they may not notice immediate gains but that their sophomore, junior, and senior GPA may benefit from these efforts during the first year) and point out the other positive outcomes of the tutoring experience.

Limitations

These results point to several areas for future research and have important implications for higher education practice and policy. However, they are limited by a few factors. First, although there are a large number of students in the sample, it is important to be clear about the generalizability of these data within and across institutions. When compared to national averages, the 2002 CIRP Freshman Survey–2003 YFCY data underrepresent both male students and students of color, particularly African American and Latino students, and evidence a slight skew toward higher-achieving students and those who attend college farther from home. In addition, there are some biases by institutional type. For example, the data underrepresent students from public universities and four-year colleges and overrepresent students from private nonsectarian and religious four-year colleges. However, since these measures were included in the blocks of input and environmental control variables (blocks one and two) and since relationships among variables tend to be robust regardless of sample representativeness, it is likely that these biases in the sample had minimal impact on the findings of the current study.

A second cautionary note concerns the nature of the dependent variables. Although the self-rated cognitive development factor is highly reliable, the items contained in it are self-rated change measures. As such, these variables may be biased in a positive direction (that is, students are likely to rate their personal skills qualities as "higher" or "much higher" than when they entered college and to underrepresent a decline in abilities). Further, while perceptions of one's performance often are related to true accomplishments, self-reported change in cognitive skills does not necessarily indicate real development.

There are similar limitations with respect to students' reports of their GPA. Most notably, the timing of survey administration (toward the end of the first year of college but before students leave for summer) and different academic calendars (for example, semester versus quarter) potentially will result in variations with respect to reporting of first-year GPA. For example, it is possible that one student may be reporting a first-year GPA from only one term, while another student from a different institution may have received grade reports more frequently. Since academic calendar and decisions with respect to timing of survey dissemination are correlated highly with institutional type, some of this bias may have been accounted for by the variables in block two, but it is likely that these items did not fully control for this potential bias. Therefore, these findings should be validated with other measures of these constructs in future research.

Although the focus of these results was on variables that remained significant to the final step with a *beta* coefficient of .05 or greater, the third limitation is evident when we examine the size of the *beta* coefficients for many of the other variables in the two regressions. Although almost all of the findings are highly significant statistically ($p < .001$), the absolute effect sizes are small for several of the first-year experience and involvement variables in each analysis. Because this study was largely an exploration of the potential relationships between college experiences and academic and intellectual development during the first year, these more modest effect sizes can be viewed as suggestive of various potential relationships. As such, they need to be investigated further in future research.

Conclusions

Although many of the results of the current study validate what one may already know intuitively, empirical evidence can help institute campus policy with respect to the structure, requirements, and pedagogies used in first-year courses and the nature and content of academic resources used by first-year students. Given the shrinking budgets of state legislatures and empty coffers on individual campuses, it is critical for campus decision makers to have assessment data to help guide campus fiscal and human resources.

For example, these findings are a valuable reminder to faculty, academic advisors, and staff that in order to help students achieve higher grades, they should design first-year programs and classroom practices that empower students to participate in class, facilitate their engagement with the material, and enhance students' feelings of satisfaction with academic experiences, particularly those related to classroom instruction and relevancy of the coursework. Since many first-year courses are large, represent required general education

NEW DIRECTIONS FOR STUDENT SERVICES • DOI: 10.1002/ss

curriculum, and employ formal lectures, these classroom experiences tend not to be especially engaging. Findings from the current research argue for smaller, more engaging classes for first-year students. In view of the fact that enrolling in an honors course is another significant predictor of GPA, this type of experience may provide an important model for classroom practices and support structures to facilitate these first-year experiences that enhance students' grades. Further, academic advisors can encourage first-year students to enroll in courses designed to engage them more fully and to dispel the common myth that students should load up on general education courses early in their academic career in order to get their requirements "out of the way" (Light, 2001).

The current research also suggests specific ways that campus personnel can enhance students' perceptions of their cognitive development. Since first-year students' feelings of satisfaction with academic experiences is the strongest predictor common to both outcome variables, it is a natural issue to include in strategic planning initiatives as well as a place to invest fiscal and human resources. It is also critical for campus personnel who work with first-year students to create a campus environment that includes meaningful and inspirational content in the curriculum, to dedicate resources to enhance students' satisfaction with academic facilities, to set high expectations and establish support structures for students to spend ample time studying and doing homework, and to create opportunities for students to collaborate and discuss courses outside of the classroom. This last finding is a particularly valuable reminder to faculty that they should support academic collaboration and teach undergraduates to treat each other as colleagues rather than competitors. Efforts to encourage students to work together on homework and readings and even to assign group projects are important to students' perceptions of their cognitive development.

As one reflects on these areas that have important implications for students' academic and cognitive growth, one must also consider patterns of student behavior and involvement with respect to these activities. For example, although academic disengagement is a predictor of both outcomes, albeit a weak one for self-assessed cognitive development by the final step of the equation, previous research shows that students are entering college with a history of low levels of academic involvement. Moreover, extensive descriptive analyses with these data show that academic disengagement persists throughout the first year of college. Further, results of frequency distributions indicate that there is also room for improvement for aspects of students' satisfaction with certain academic experiences and facilities, including the relevance of coursework and academic advising. These are just a few examples that suggest than many first-year students are missing out on the positive outcomes associated with certain college activities, including the gains identified in this research. Since these gains often are theoretically linked to critical stages of intellectual growth and cognitive development, the results here represent a call to arms for campus personnel.

NEW DIRECTIONS FOR STUDENT SERVICES • DOI: 10.1002/ss

Identifying the first-year experiences that are related to the desired academic outcomes of college without making a commitment to action on the institutional and national level does not help advance the field of higher education or move us closer to achieving our ultimate goal of educating students and creating a foundation for their future development. Assessment of student experiences ideally should represent a feedback channel for higher education professionals and decision makers to capitalize on the student responses to the assessment effort. Findings such as those presented in the current study are most effective when they are actually used to enact policy, to develop programs, and to channel resources where they are most needed and have the potential to be most effective. The bottom line is that the full potential of assessment efforts and the data that emerge from them is achieved only when they are used both to assess the needs of first-year students, and to evaluate the ways in which campus programs and pedagogies meet these needs, and then are translated into campus policies meant to ease students' transition to college and to enhance institutional impact on student outcomes. Only then are we attending to the true mission of higher education.

References

Astin, A. W. *Achieving Educational Excellence: A Critical Assessment of Priorities and Practices in Higher Education.* San Francisco: Jossey-Bass, 1985.

Astin, A. W. *Assessment for Excellence.* New York: Macmillan, 1991.

Astin, A. W. *What Matters in College.* San Francisco: Jossey-Bass, 1993.

Astin, A. W., Oseguera, L., Sax, L. J., and Korn, W. S., *The American Freshman: Thirty Year Trends.* Los Angeles, Calif.: Higher Education Research Institute, University of California at Los Angeles, 2002.

Baxter Magolda, M. B. *Knowing and Reasoning in College: Gender-Related Patterns in Students' Intellectual Development.* San Francisco: Jossey-Bass, 1992.

Bowen, H. R. *Investment in Learning: The Individual and Social Value of American Higher Education.* San Francisco: Jossey-Bass, 1977.

Cohen, A. M. *The Shaping of American Higher Education: Emergence and Growth of the Contemporary System.* San Francisco: Jossey-Bass, 1998.

Erickson, B. L., and Strommer, D. W. *Teaching College Freshmen.* San Francisco: Jossey-Bass, 1991.

Evans, N. J., Forney, D. S., and Guido-DiBrito, F. *Student Development in College: Theory, Research, and Practice.* San Francisco: Jossey-Bass, 1998.

Feldman, K. A., and Newcomb, T. M. *The Impact of College on Students.* San Francisco: Jossey-Bass, 1969.

Goodchild, L. F., and Wechsler, H. S. *The History of Higher Education.* (2nd ed.) (ASHE Reader Series). Boston, Mass.: Pearson Custom Publishing, 1997.

Keup, J. R., and Stolzenberg, E. B. *The 2003 Your First College Year (YFCY) Survey: Exploring the Academic and Personal Experiences of First-Year Students* (monograph no. 40). Columbia, S.C.: National Resource Center for The First-Year Experience and Students in Transition, University of South Carolina, 2004.

Kuh, G. D., Schuh, J. H., Whitt, E. J., and Associates. *Involving Colleges: Successful Approaches to Fostering Student Learning and Development Outside the Classroom.* San Francisco: Jossey-Bass, 1991.

Kurfiss, J. G. "Critical Thinking: Theory Research, and Possibilities." *ASHE-ERIC Higher Education Report*. Washington, D.C.: Association for the Study of Higher Education, 1988.

Light, R. J. *Making the Most of College: Students Speak Their Minds*. Cambridge, Mass: Harvard University Press, 2001.

Lucas, C. J. *American Higher Education: A History*. New York: St. Martin's Press, 1994.

Pascarella, E. T., and Terenzini, P. T. *How College Affects Students: Findings and Insights from Twenty Years of Research*. San Francisco: Jossey-Bass, 1991.

Pascarella, E. T., and Terenzini, P. T. *How College Affects Students: A Third Decade of Research*. San Francisco: Jossey-Bass, 2005.

Pedhazur, E. J. *Multiple Regression in Behavioral Research: Explanation and Prediction*. (3rd ed.). New York: Harcourt Brace College Publishers, 1997.

Perry, W .G. "Cognitive and Ethical Growth: The Making of Meaning." In A. W. Chickering and Associates (eds.), *The Modern American College: Responding to the New Realities of Diverse Students and a Changing Society*. San Francisco: Jossey-Bass, 1981.

Sax, L. J., and others. *Findings from the 2002 Administration of Your First College Year (YFCY): National Aggregates*. Los Angeles, Calif.: Higher Education Research Institute, University of California at Los Angeles, 2002.

Schilling, K. M., and Schilling, K. L. "Increasing Expectations for Student Effort." *About Campus*, 1999, 4(2), 4–10.

Schilling, K. M., and Schilling, K. L. "Expectations and Performance." In M. L. Upcraft, J. N. Gardner, B. O. Barefoot, and Associates (eds.), *Challenging and Supporting the First-Year Student: A Handbook for Improving the First Year of College*. San Francisco: Jossey-Bass, 2005.

Upcraft, M. L., Gardner, J. N., and Associates. *The Freshman Year Experience: Helping Students Survive and Succeed in College*. San Francisco: Jossey-Bass, 1989.

JENNIFER R. KEUP is principal research analyst for the Student Affairs Information and Research Office (SAIRO) at the University of California at Los Angeles.

NEW DIRECTIONS FOR STUDENT SERVICES • DOI: 10.1002/ss

Hispanics are the fastest-growing ethnic population in the United States. This chapter presents demographic projections for higher education and discusses the role of the transfer function in community colleges. Two notable transfer programs are highlighted.

Who Will We Serve in the Future? The New Student in Transition

Jaime Lester

Although there are many educational transitions throughout life, moving grade levels and educational sectors—that is, the transition of transferring from a two-year to a four-year institution—is noted as one where students are found to experience the most difficulty. For this reason, this chapter focuses on the singular transition of transfer. Many transfer students take less linear paths, transferring back to a two-year institution from a four-year one, termed "reverse transfer" (Kajstura and Keim, 1992). For the purposes of this chapter, however, transfer is defined as applying only to students who move from a two-year to a four-year institution. The rate of transfer between two- and four-year institutions is estimated at approximately 25 percent nationally (Cohen and Brawer, 2003), with countless variations by individual institutions. Approximately six million students attend the nation's community colleges, making transfer a significant avenue to a bachelor's degree. The typical transfer student is a white, twenty-six-year-old female who works part-time (Fredrickson, 1998). After earning the required credits, she persists and transfers to a four-year institution, earning a bachelor's degree two or three years later.

The profile of the typical transfer student will change dramatically over the next ten to fifteen years to reflect population and demographic shifts. Population increases, coupled with educational budget cuts forcing higher educational institutions to decrease the number of available seats, will alter postsecondary access. A larger number of students, higher tuition, and the decreasing availability of seats in four-year institutions create a specific

New Directions for Student Services, no. 114, Summer 2006 © Wiley Periodicals, Inc.
Published online in Wiley InterScience (www.interscience.wiley.com) • DOI: 10.1002/ss.206

47

environment where highly capable students are unable to gain access to the more competitive and costly four-year institutions. In addition, the demographic and population changes are moving in directions never before seen in the United States. The Hispanic population is continuing to grow, surpassing the white population in several urban cities including Los Angeles (Llagas, 2003). More highly qualified students will seek out community colleges, aspiring to transfer to a college or university later, with notable demographic shifts that affect the institutional culture and service needs throughout higher education.

I begin by outlining the population and demographic projections for the higher education system in the United States, with a focus on the Hispanic population as one of the fastest-growing population segments. I then present a case study of California that highlights state-level concerns arising from these demographic changes. Following is a review of the research on transfer. Finally, I outline two notable programs currently providing successful transitional services and offer suggestions for institutions and student affairs professionals pertaining to the development of transitional programs for students seeking the transfer option. In the coming years, the demographic and population changes in the United States will affect higher education in new ways. As a result, demand for programs that assist students seeking to transfer from two-year to four-year institutions will increase.

The Future Demographic Landscape of Education

Recent population projections indicate that the population of the United States is rising. In the current decade, the estimated number of individuals who live in the United States and Puerto Rico increased by approximately thirty million people (U.S. Census, 2004). Since the number of births each year is not static, the steady increase of births creates more use of public services. Education, as one of these public services, is affected dramatically by population trends. To account for the increases in the number of students eligible for postsecondary education, colleges and universities must continue to grow. However, decreased state appropriations to higher education place institutions in a double bind; that is, they are trying to serve more students with less money.

Not all institutions of higher education are affected equally by population growth. As the only tier of the higher educational hierarchy with an open-door admissions policy, community colleges continue to experience larger increases in the number of students seeking admission than do their four-year counterparts. At first glance, increases in educational enrollment seem positive—more individuals seeking postsecondary degrees or certificates contribute to an educated populace in the current postindustrial economy. However, problems arise when enrollment exceeds capacity and institutional budgets are stretched too thin. Educational programs and services at both the federal and state levels are continuous targets for federal and state budget reductions, leaving institutions with more students and less money. While four-year universities can raise tuition and increase admission standards, community colleges must maintain adherence to their open-door policy.

Population trends in the United States greatly affect the educational system. Each year, millions of children are born in the United States, most of whom will enter primary school five years later and continue through secondary education. Native-born children are not the only individuals populating the educational system. Each year, approximately one million immigrants enter the United States (U.S. Citizenship and Immigration Services, 2004). The majority of them reside in California, New York, and Texas and are afforded the opportunity to enroll in postsecondary institutions. The National Center for Education Statistics projects that by 2015, total postsecondary enrollments will rise by 19 percent, with a 21 percent increase for women and 15 percent for men. Private institutions will experience slightly larger increases of 20 percent compared to 18 percent for public institutions (National Center for Education Statistics, 2003).

In terms of actual student numbers, conservative estimates indicate that colleges and universities are likely to see an increase of more than two million students by 2015 (Education Commission of the States, 2005). To match the current college participation rates in the best-performing states, postsecondary access nationwide would need to expand by more than ten million students (Education Commission of the States, 2005). Institutions, however, will not have an opportunity to cut per-student costs. Current fund expenditures for both two-year and four-year students are expected to increase to $10,800 and $30,800 per full-time equivalent student, respectively (National Center for Education Statistics, 2003).

These figures are of particular interest, as state governments increasingly are considering and enacting budgetary cuts to both secondary and postsecondary public education. For example, Governor Arnold Schwarzenegger's California State Budget proposal outlines significant cuts to higher education, including a 10 percent decrease in the number of seats available at state-supported four-year institutions and a budget cut of $29.9 million for the University of California system in 2004 (State of California, 2004).

Hispanic Population. By 2010, the Hispanic population in the United States is expected to become the largest minority group in the country, surpassing the African American population (Llagas, 2003). By 2015, whites will make up only 58 percent of those in the under-twenty-four age range. At the same time, the Hispanic population of the same age range is expected to nearly double, from 12 percent in 1990 to 21 percent in 2015; half of all school children will be non-Anglo American by 2025 (Education Commission of the States, 2005). The Hispanic population is younger, on average, than the population overall (Llagas, 2003). This is the population that will be entering the higher education system by 2015. Although the Hispanic population varies by state and is clustered primarily in California, New York, and Texas, this racial and ethnic shift has the potential to affect all states and is therefore the focus of this chapter.

Despite the demographic increase in Hispanics throughout the United States, disparities still exist in postsecondary enrollment. Hispanics account for 14 percent of students enrolled in two-year institutions and 7 percent of those in four-year institutions (National Center for Education Statistics, 2003). Hispanic-serving institutions, however, account for a large proportion of Hispanic student enrollment—45 percent of full-time Hispanic students are enrolled in such institutions. Although Hispanics seem to be faring better than in previous years, as evidenced by the fact that they are enrolling in postsecondary institutions at greater rates, much of the enrollment occurs in the institutions that continuously serve large proportions of Hispanic students. It is possible that access is segregated to particular institutions: those that offer a two-year curriculum and those that are classified as two- and four-year Hispanic-serving institutions.

Of notable concern are the small percentages of Hispanics between the ages of twenty-five and twenty-nine graduating from four-year programs. In 2000, only 10 percent of Hispanics earned a bachelor's degree, compared to 34 percent of whites and 18 percent of blacks (National Center for Education Statistics, 2003). However, these statistics do not capture Hispanic participation in other types of postsecondary education. Hispanics are more likely to participate in adult education that has a career or vocational track (National Center for Education Statistics, 2003). Hispanics may not be participating in academic programs at the same rates as other racial or ethnic groups, but they continue to seek out vocational educational experiences that have a quick return on investment. Despite Hispanics' comparatively low levels of participation in academic programs, research shows that more Hispanic students are taking advanced placement courses, signaling a potential increase in postsecondary participation in future generations (Llagas, 2003).

Economic Factors. It appears as if the overall increase in enrollment will be attributed entirely to population changes. However, other economic changes affect individual decision making regarding postsecondary attendance. The rising demand is due equally to the need to establish economic self-sufficiency when manufacturing jobs are located in other countries and service-sector jobs fail to pay living wages (Education Commission of the States, 2005). A postsecondary degree or certificate is the gateway to jobs that allow for economic stability. In fact, students who receive a bachelor's degree will earn, on average, one million dollars more in a lifetime than a high school graduate (U.S. Census, 2004). These estimates alone underscore the need for a postsecondary degree or certificate to create access to the middle-class standard of living provided by skilled jobs.

In addition to the economic advantages of a postsecondary education, higher levels of education are also necessary to participate fully in a democratic government (Education Commission of the States, 2005). Increasing participation in the democratic process—including learning and understanding candidate platforms—relies on a higher level of education. The emergence of new voting practices requiring technological savvy, such as voting on the Internet, and an increased reliance on Internet Web sites to communicate candidate positions, presupposes a certain level of computer skills. The importance of postsecondary degrees and certificates for jobs as well as democratic participation is an additional reason that higher education will continue to attract unprecedented numbers of students.

The Case of California

To underscore the importance of population trends on the education system and to illustrate the complexities of disaggregated demographic trends, California serves as an appropriate case study. California has one of the largest systems of postsecondary education in the United States. With more than one hundred community colleges and thirty-three California State and University of California institutions, more than two million students are enrolled in California's higher education system each year (State of California, 2003). California is also experiencing significant demographic changes. Estimates indicate that by 2015, the proportion of California's population between eighteen and twenty-four years old is expected to increase by 11.4 percent (Western Interstate Commission for Higher Education, 2005).

The growth in the population disproportionately affects community colleges. In 2002, California community colleges registered one in four postsecondary students, California State University (CSU) campuses one in six, and University of California (UC) campuses one in twelve (State of California, 2003). If community colleges maintain current enrollment trends, by 2012 their student population is expected to grow nearly 20 percent, or by 346,000 students (State of California, 2003). Further complicating the postsecondary situation in California is the ailing state budget, which is undergoing dramatic changes with regard to cutbacks in education, forcing tuition increases and generating discussion of decreasing postsecondary capacity. This dilemma should not come as a surprise. In 1996 the RAND Corporation projected that access levels to postsecondary education in California would decrease dramatically by 2010, leaving more than one million students underserved (Shires, 1996).

California also provides an important context in which to examine the changing racial and ethnic composition of the United States. Among the 6,298,769 students in California's public primary and secondary schools, 46 percent are Hispanic and 32.5 percent are white (State of California, 2005). Many of the Hispanic students entering the California public schools are not academically competitive. Each year approximately 350,000 students graduate from the public school system in California. Of those, only 26 percent of Hispanics complete the course requirements to apply to public four-year institutions. The white population fares better, with 44 percent of the students having completed the course requirements (Tornatzky, Torres, and Caswell,

NEW DIRECTIONS FOR STUDENT SERVICES • DOI: 10.1002/ss

2003). When looking at high school degree completion using a cohort model, 41 percent, or approximately thirty thousand Hispanic students, drop out between ninth and twelfth grades (Tornatzky, Torres, and Caswell, 2003). The small numbers of high school completers, coupled with a disproportionate number of students who complete the requirements for admission to a four-year university, results in a disproportionately small representation of Hispanic students in postsecondary education—only 24.1 percent.

Transfer as the Transition

Transfer students need specific forms of assistance so that they may complete the course requirements at the two-year institution and then transition into the four-year institution successfully. The demographic composition of transfer students varies by state, yet many of the transfer students are found to be older, female, and Caucasian, In some cities, such as Los Angeles, where the population is predominately Latino, transfer students are more likely to be of Latino ethnicity. The National Study of Student Engagement (2003) found that transfer students believe that coursework is essential to higher-order thinking, spend more time preparing for class, but tend to be less engaged in educational activities. They tend also to have more external responsibilities, such as working off campus or raising a family. The multiple responsibilities result in students who typically live off campus and have fewer interactions with faculty members. Consistently, transfer students note low levels of satisfaction with the campus climate and with relationships with peers and faculty.

Academic concerns. Gardner and Barefoot (1995) note that transfer students commonly face issues involving both academic and social concerns. Academic concerns include academic skills and performance, faculty-student interaction, and advising and planning; social concerns include involvement and adjustment to college, finances, and level of self-efficacy. Other researchers note that the differences in institutional size, location, academic rigor, and competition among students are among the reasons that transfer students have difficulty transitioning to four-year institutions (Laanan, 1996, 1998, 2001). Still other researchers emphasize the importance of finances as one of many barriers facing transfer students who are transferring to four-year institutions (McDonough, 1997).

Financial concerns. The difference in cost from attending a community college is a factor students must consider in transferring to a four-year institution. In Los Angeles, for example, community college tuition is $18 per credit unit. At the California State Universities, student tuition is based on either part-time or full-time status. Part-time undergraduate students (taking up to six units or semester credit hours) pay a state university fee of $1,356 per academic year. Full-time students (taking more than six units) pay a state university fee of $2,334. In addition, students normally pay campus-based fees (for the student association, health fees, and other services), which currently average $582 per year. Comparing the nominal $18 per credit to a cost of at least $1,356 for the four-year state schools, it is clear that individuals need to consider the additional cost for tuition and fees when transferring to a four-year institution.

Grades. The adjustment process for transfer students is complex; performance, perceived value of education, and academic and social integration are all significant factors in the success of transfer students (Laanan, 2001). Even more complex is the measurable result of the adjustment process. It must be noted, however, that not all students experience difficulties in the transfer process, and the difficulties they do encounter do not always result in negative outcomes. Laanan (2001) notes that transfer shock (a decrease in grade-point average [GPA] after enrollment in a four-year institution) is smaller than previously noted. Drops in students' GPAs are less than one-half of a grade point (Laanan, 2001). Students who enter a four-year institution with a GPA of 3.5, for example, typically earn a GPA of not lower than 3.0 (on a four-point scale) at the end of the first semester.

Students who are the most successful during the inherent transition in the transfer process are those who are best informed and have most actively prepared for transfer (Berger and Malaney, 2003). These students have been academically counseled throughout the process and understand the procedures of transfer as well as the environment and academic standards they are transferring to. An important fact is that many of the more successful transfer students have also had opportunities to visit the four-year institution to gain a perspective on the campus environment. In addition, these successful students have maintained family relationships and support networks, facilitating adjustment to college (Hurtado, Carter, and Spuler, 1996).

Ethnic differences. The description of adjustment difficulties and factors that promote success for the transfer student assumes a homogeneous student population. In fact, racial and ethnic minorities encounter additional stressors during transfer (Laanan, 2001). The demographic composition and social climate on the campus can be a source of stress. For example, Hispanic students who attended predominately Hispanic community colleges, which is the typical case for California, may have difficulties adjusting to a predominately white student body at a four-year institution. Rendon and Valadez (1993) found that Hispanic students encounter particular difficulties in the transfer process that potentially hinder degree attainment at senior institutions. Specifically, family, finances, knowledge of the transfer process and the four-year institution system, relationships with administrators and faculty at both the community college and senior-level institutions, and, most important, cultural understanding all affect educational success for Hispanic transfer students. Haralson (1996) notes that students of color may perceive primarily white institutions to be exclusive and lacking commitment to fostering cultural pluralism, multicultural curriculum, and campus diversity.

NEW DIRECTIONS FOR STUDENT SERVICES • DOI: 10.1002/ss

Institutional Response

In this chapter, I have outlined the changing demographics of the United States that indicate an increase in students seeking postsecondary education in the years to come. The number of seats available at four-year institutions will continue to shrink, forcing more students into the open access of community colleges. Increasing numbers of students of Hispanic origin will seek opportunities to transfer. This crucial juncture of transfer offers special challenges, with a continuous need for support in the form of both institutional and community involvement. To help these students succeed, institutional intervention is necessary and influential. Hurtado and Carter (1997) outlined several studies noting that early transition experiences in the form of peer groups and college adjustment interventions have the potential to assist in student transfer success and can be facilitated by institutional intervention. Despite the potential for institutions to organize intervention strategies and programs promoting student transfer success, senior institutions are making only minimal efforts to address the needs of transfer students. In a study conducted by Swing (2000), only one-third of the campuses reported having programs specifically designed for transfer students. The programs that currently exist include transfer student liaisons, peer advising groups, summer institutes, and orientation programs.

Several techniques are important when evaluating or designing transfer programs. Watson (2000) noted that programs need to be of assistance at multiple student transition points, including the transition from high school to community college, and should begin targeting students early, such as in elementary school. Other researchers note the importance of considering the demographic composition, enrollment patterns, and academic backgrounds of students when designing support programs for transfer students (Fredrickson, 1998). Certainly, with the large numbers of Hispanic students who will enter community colleges hoping to transition to four-year institutions, support programs must focus on the particular needs of these students.

Transfer programs have emerged across the United States. In the remainder of this chapter, I highlight two programs: the Puente Project in California, and the Georgia P-16 Initiative.

The Puente Project

Established in 1981 by an English professor and an academic counselor at Chabot Community College in Hayward, California, the Puente Project seeks to increase the number of educationally disadvantaged students in both high schools and community colleges. Hailed as one of the most effective programs in the United States by a consortium of educational associations and leaders, the Puente Project has experienced enormous success by embracing social, cultural, and differential learning styles in developing learning communities. These communities are found in fifty-six community colleges

New Directions for Student Services • DOI: 10.1002/ss

across California. The Puente Project is open to all students, but consistently serves a large majority of Hispanic students due to the demographics of California and the low levels of academic success experienced by Hispanics.

The design of the project shows a multilevel approach. First, on an academic level, students are placed in accelerated English writing courses, with a focus on Mexican and Latino literature and experiences. By using ethnic-oriented literature, the project addresses the specific cultural and social contexts, affirming student differences and diversity. Second, students meet with an academic counselor regularly to assist with college applications, the transfer process from community college to four-year institutions, and financial aid applications. Many of California's community colleges suffer from high student-to-counselor ratios, with one counselor for every one thousand students. Having an opportunity to meet with a counselor on a regular basis is invaluable for these students. Third, the project pairs each student with a mentor, usually a successful community leader, to serve as an advisor and example of success. Finally, the students attend field trips to various college campuses. Having an opportunity to see college campuses demystifies the college experience and assists students in navigating through the landscape of buildings.

Puente students are consistently more successful than their non-Puente peers. More than 47 percent of Puente community college students transfer to four-year universities and colleges, compared to 27 percent of non-Puente students (Puente Project, 2005). The large majority, 90 percent, of the students in the Puente project persist after the first year, and 73 percent persist after the second year (Puente Project, 2005). Although it is difficult to track community college students due to their "stop out" behavior, persistence estimates for non-Puente students are far lower than those for students in the Puente program. The Puente Project incorporates culture and social contexts along with consistent institutional support and involvement to assist primarily Hispanic students to succeed. As the next case illustrates, support from leaders on multiple levels of education is also important for student success

Georgia P-16 Initiative

The next example describes an initiative in Georgia to systematically change the educational system to a P-16 focus. Although this case broadens the topic of transition from two-year to four-year institutions, it provides an example of how a system can change to accommodate students as they undergo multiple educational transitions. In addition, the Georgia initiative describes how accountability measures can be developed to aid in student transitions. Community colleges and four-year institutions may take not of how a P-16 focus and programs to promote successful transitions on all levels of education are transportable to the transfer progress.

In 1995, Governor Zell Miller of Georgia created a thirty-eight-member council charged with improving educational success for Georgia's students at all levels of education (Pathways to College Network, 2005). The governor assumed that a segregated educational system with little to no collaboration among elementary, secondary, and postsecondary schools was creating a leaky educational pipeline. Students were found to exit the educational system at the leaky transition points between high school and college, persistence in college, and transfer from two- to four-year institutions. The governor and other state officials believed that a lack of alignment among standards, expectations, and outcomes among the various levels of the educational system contributed to the leaky pipeline. To address the concern of student participation, the governor created a multiphase consortium with a range of initiatives to improve partnerships on the state level (Pathways to College Network, 2005). This group was charged with the responsibility of aligning resources and goals that would lead to student educational success. The long-term goals of the council were to improve academic achievement for all students, help students with the transition between educational sectors, ensure that postsecondary students entered academically prepared with the tools for success, and close educational attainment gaps between majority and minority populations.

To achieve these long-term goals and organize a large-scale statewide effort, the first task was the creation of a council, which was charged with creating an operational plan. Once the plan was formulated, the council disbanded and a senior advocacy group began the task of operationalizing the plan. The P-16 plan included the development of standards for all levels of education—pre-school through postsecondary levels; the creation of a common student database; linking curriculum on all levels of education; and reform efforts for programs that train teachers, school leaders, and personnel. In the third and final phase, the advocacy group created a series of subcommittees to assist in recommending operational plans. The recommendations were forwarded by the advocacy group to the appropriate educational groups, such as the department of education, for review and implementation. These subcommittees, as well as the advocacy group, all operated on a state level to facilitate cross-institutional efforts. It is important to describe the logistics of the Georgia council, as statewide efforts are consistently circumvented by bureaucracies and the sheer size of the undertaking. Understanding how Georgia was able to organize a statewide educational initiative can assist other states that are considering large-scale changes.

The results from the implementation of the P-16 Council have been encouraging. Originally, six grants were awarded to support the implementation of reform plans, with a total of nineteen grants awarded by 2000. Through the work of the council and the reform grants, Georgia has aligned standards for high school exit exams and college entrance exams to create accountability measures that ensure that graduating high school seniors are academically prepared for college. In addition, reform measures have created programs to improve the preparation of teachers to encourage academically rigorous curriculum in elementary and secondary education. In the postsecondary environment, the reform efforts have targeted undergraduate education to improve educational quality. Finally, Georgia has been successful, through the alignment of higher academic standards, in beginning to close the gap between educational attainment of minority and majority populations. For these reasons, Georgia's program has also been recognized as one of the exemplary programs in the United States by the Pathways to College consortium (Pathways to College Network, 2005). It serves as a model for other states that want to align multiple educational sectors that assist transition students throughout the educational pipeline.

While the Puente Project and the Georgia P-16 Council are just two examples of countless successful programs, each aspires to similar goals by employing differing approaches. The Puente Project seeks to address educational needs on the individual level by targeting students who have been underserved traditionally and have low levels of educational success. The individual focus allows the Puente Project to incorporate a cultural curriculum and one-on-one counseling to address specific needs of the student. Although the Puente Project has received notable success, it has yet to stimulate widespread and systematic change.

The Georgia P-16 Council is purposefully addressing the systemic change required to align multiple sectors of education. It focuses on blanket policies to create standards and accountability measures in the aggregate. The council also has received notable success, decreasing educational gaps and promoting educational success for all students. Each initiative has its merits. But the question still remains: What programs will assist large numbers of potential transfer students of Hispanic origin? Each of these initiatives offers insight into the design and implementation of programs for the future.

Suggestions for Practice

For anyone involved in the postsecondary environment for more than a few years, the ebb and flow of enrollment patterns and generational differences are not uncommon. Certainly, throughout its history, higher education has experienced moments of growth and decline. This chapter highlights changes on the horizon for higher education to provoke administrators and student affairs professionals to consider designing programs for transfer students. The transition of transferring from a community college to a four-year institution is one of the most important educational transitions in a student's life. Many students face academic difficulties, cultural confusion, and social uncertainty. Students experience transfer shock, as exhibited in a small but important decrease in grade-point averages. Hispanic students have particular difficulties in finances and assimilation into a less culturally conscious environment. Understanding the specific difficulties of Hispanic students is crucial, since projected patterns of enrollment predict an increase in Hispanic students and transfer students regardless of race. In addition to the demand of transfer students, higher education also will see a renewed interest in colleges and universities as a transitional environment from living in the parental home to entering the workforce.

NEW DIRECTIONS FOR STUDENT SERVICES • DOI: 10.1002/ss

The two exemplar programs, the Puente Project and Georgia's P-16 Council, provide examples of successful programs on two different levels: individual and statewide. The Puente Project specifically assists individual students in transferring successfully, and Georgia's P-16 Council focuses on systemic reforms across educational sectors. Although transfer students within the Georgia P-16 reforms are not targeted specifically, they benefit from the curricular and support services designed to connect each educational sector. Table 4.1 details the demographic changes that will affect the educational system in the United States, the specific empirical findings of the challenges of transfer students, and a list of recommendations to consider when designing programs to assist new transfer students.

Conclusion

The growing population of diverse transfer students poses a challenge for postsecondary administrators and students affairs professionals. The likely

Table 4.1. Considerations for Community College Transfer Students.

Demographic	Transfer Considerations	Programmatic Considerations
• Increase in the enrollment of Hispanic students • More students seeking to transfer who are academically capable	• Transfer shock—more rigorous coursework in four-year colleges and universities • Campus geographically larger and difficult to navigate • Paying for increased tuition costs • Competition among students • Academic advising for students new to the four-year curriculum • Facilitation of faculty-student interaction • Specific cultural differences between the two-year and four-year institution • Successful transfer students are well informed and academically prepared	• Cultural curriculum or course content • Small-group setting • Frequent academic advising • Connections with former and new institution • Mentoring • Multiple levels of reform • Consistent academic preparation in the K-12 sector for all groups • Relationships among all sectors of education • Statewide reform grants to foster partnerships

increase of Hispanic students fueled by population changes and the continually decreasing number of seats in four-year institutions will limit access, forcing many students to enter four-year institutions from community colleges. Transfer students have particular concerns that are far different from those of native students. The initial few months after transfer are stressful for students as they acclimate to a new environment. Transfer students have difficulty paying high tuition costs, navigating a larger campus, and coping with more rigorous academic standards. Most important, students from diverse racial or ethnic backgrounds often find the campus culture to be unwelcoming and uncomfortable. Each of these challenges highlights a need to create and evaluate programs that assist transfer students in finding educational success in the four-year environment.

It is important for student affairs professionals and university administrators to consider curriculum and content that are culturally based. As seen with the Puente Project, using resources that are relevant to the Hispanic population has assisted in student success. Small-group settings with frequent academic advising facilitate peer and professional advisement and support, which are crucial for students who are undergoing a change from community colleges to four-year institutions. On a macro level, institutions also need to consider how statewide groups can assist in facilitating cooperation across multiple levels of education. Programs that overlap educational sectors have the potential to help students manage the transition from one institution to another more easily. Imagine a transfer program with faculty and staff from the four-year institution housed in the community college. Students would have an opportunity to interact with four-year institutional representatives regularly before they enter the new institution. Statewide efforts can assist both financially and legislatively in supporting new programs that transcend institutional boundaries.

Student populations have and will continue to undergo countless changes. Individuals who have worked in higher education for many years have seen such changes. These changes in student population require action to successfully design support services to assist these students. The considerations listed above are a few ideas to begin these necessary conversations. All students deserve assistance, regardless of the point at which they enter the higher education institution. Meeting the needs of the new transfer student population will require thinking outside of the box, using valuable campus resources to help them walk down the aisle and receive the all-important bachelor's degree.

References

Berger, J. B., and Malaney, G. D. "Assessing the Transition to Transfer Students from Community College to a University." *NASPA Journal*, 2003, 40(4), 1–23.

Cohen, A. M., and Brawer, F. B. *The American Community College.* (4th ed.) San Francisco: Jossey-Bass, 2003.

Education Commission of the States. *ECS Issue Site: Demographics*, 2005. http://www.ecs.org/html/IssueSection. Accessed Apr. 5, 2005.

Fredrickson, J. "Today's Transfer Students: Who Are They?" *Community College Review*, 1998, 26(1), 43–54.

Gardner, J. N., and Barefoot, B. O. "Investigating the Experience of Transfer Students." Unpublished manuscript, University of South Carolina at Columbia, 1995.

Haralson, M., Jr. *Survival Factors for Black Students in Predominately White Campuses*. Paper presented at the annual meeting of the National Association of Student Personnel Administrators, Atlanta, Ga., 1996.

Hurtado, S., Carter, D. F., and Spuler, A. J. "Latino Student Transition to College: Assessing Difficulties and Factors in Successful Adjustment." *Research in Higher Education*, 1996, 37, 135–157.

Hurtado, S., and Carter, D. F. "Effects of College Transition and Perceptions of the Campus Racial Climate on Latino College Students' Sense of Belonging." *Sociology of Education*, 1997, 70, 324–345.

Kajstura, A., and Keim, M. C. "Reverse Transfer Students in Illinois Community College." *Community College Review*, 1992, 20(2), 39–44.

Laanan, F. S. "Making the Transition: Understanding the Adjustment Process of Community College Transfer Students." *Community College Review*, 1996, 23(4), 69–84.

Laanan, F. S. "Beyond Transfer Shock: A Study of Students' College Experiences and Adjustment Process at UCLA." Unpublished doctoral dissertation, Graduate School of Education and Information Studies, University of California, Los Angeles, 1998.

Laanan, F. S. "Transfer Student Adjustment." In F. S. Laanan (ed.), *Transfer Students: Trends and Issues*. New Directions for Community Colleges, no. 114. San Francisco: Jossey-Bass, 2001.

Llagas, C. "Status and Trends in the Education of Hispanics." *Education Statistics Quarterly*, 2003, 5(2).

McDonough, P. M. *Choosing Colleges: How Social Class and Schools Structure Opportunity*. Albany: State University of New York Press, 1997.

National Center for Education Statistics. "Projections of Education Statistics to 2013," 2003. http://nces.ed.gov/programs/projections/ch_7.asp. Accessed Apr. 5, 2005.

National Study of Student Engagement. *The College Student Report: 2003 Overview*. Bloomington: Indiana University, 2003.

Pathways to College Network. "Georgia P-16 Initiatives, University System of Georgia," 2005. http://www.pathwaystocollege.net/webarticles/pdf/georgiap16.pdf. Accessed March 24, 2005.

Puente Project. "Bridge to a Better Future: A State of the Program Report from the Puente Project," 2005. http://www.puente.net/. Accessed Mar. 24, 2005.

Rendon, L. I., and Valadez, J. R. "Qualitative Indicators of Hispanic Student Transfer." *Community College Review*, 1993, 20(4), 27–37.

Shires, M. A. *The Future of Public Undergraduate Education in California*. Santa Monica: RAND, 1996.

State of California. *California Postsecondary Enrollment Projections, 2003*. Sacramento: Department of Finance, 2003.

State of California. *California Budget for 2004–2005: Higher Education*, 2004. Sacramento: Department of Finance, 2004. http://www.dof.ca.gov/HTML/Budgt04–05/BudgetSum04/High_Ed_w.pdf. Accessed Mar. 24, 2005.

State of California. "State of California Education Profile: Fiscal Year 2003–04," 2005. http://www.ed-data.k12.ca.us/profile.asp. Accessed Apr. 5, 2005.

Swing, R. L. *Transfer Student Support Programs*. Policy Center on the First Year of College. Brevard, NC: Brevard College, 2000.

Tornatzky, L. G., Torres, C., and Caswell, T. *Latino Scorecard: Grading the American Dream 2003*. Los Angeles, Calif.: Tomas Rivera Policy Institute, 2003.

U.S. Bureau of the Census. "California Quick Facts," 2004. http://quickfacts.census.gov/qfd/states/06000.html. Accessed Apr. 25, 2005.

U.S. Citizenship and Immigration Services. Office of Immigrations Statistics. "2003 Yearbook of Immigration Statistics," 2004. http://uscis.gov/graphics/shared/statistics/yearbook/2003/2003Yearbook.pdf. Accessed Apr. 25, 2005.

Watson, L. "Working with Schools to Ease Student Transition to the Community College." In J. C. Palmer (ed.), *How Community Colleges Can Create Productive Collaborations with Local Schools*. New Directions for Community Colleges, no. 4. San Francisco: Jossey-Bass, 2000.

Western Interstate Commission for Higher Education. "California State Highlights," 2005. http://www.wiche.edu/States/ca.asp. Accessed Mar. 25, 2005.

JAIME LESTER *is a research assistant and doctoral candidate at the University of Southern California in the Rossier School of Education. Her dissertation addresses issues related to gender among faculty at community colleges.*

5

This chapter presents the changes in recent international student enrollment in American higher education and examines policy issues affecting international students' access to colleges and universities. Implications for student services are discussed.

International Students in Transition: Changes in Access to U.S. Higher Education

Soko S. Starobin

In the midst of the global terrorism threat, international educators have continued to provide access to scholars around the world to share their scholarship, cultural heritage, and language with academic communities in America's colleges and universities. Since the September 11, 2001, terrorist attacks, however, the scrutiny of international student visa applicants to academic institutions in the United States has become a major focus of America's national security. The creation of the Department of Homeland Security (DHS), followed by the implementation of the Student and Exchange Visitor Information System (SEVIS), brought numerous changes in access to institutions of higher education and challenges to those who provide assistance and support for visiting students and scholars.

Prior to the implementation of SEVIS, information on nonimmigrant students (F and M visa categories) and exchange visitors (J visa category) who enrolled in American colleges and universities was manually processed by designated school officials (DSO) at each institution. SEVIS is a Web-based data collection and reporting system that monitors how colleges and universities comply with federal regulations. SEVIS also provides more stringent scrutiny of international students and exchange visitors; thus, it has sent unwelcoming messages to the world's academic communities. During the 2003–04 academic year, the enrollment of international students at U.S. institutions of higher education declined for the first time since the Institute of

NEW DIRECTIONS FOR STUDENT SERVICES, no. 114, Summer 2006   © Wiley Periodicals, Inc.
Published online in Wiley InterScience (www.interscience.wiley.com) • DOI: 10.1002/ss.207

63

International Education began conducting a census of foreign students in the United States (Chin and Gallup-Black, 2004). Having recognized the negative consequences of SEVIS, the NAFSA Association of International Educator's Strategic Task Force on International Student Access argued that continuing the open access to international students can be "part of the solution to terrorism, not part of the problem" (2003, p. 3). Furthermore, international educators and leaders in higher education have urged DHS to make continuous improvements to the system to alleviate the negative consequences of SEVIS as well as to increase public awareness of contributions of international education to national security. These international educators and leaders in colleges and universities identified contributions of international education as helping U.S. citizens develop global understanding, advancing scientific and economic competitiveness, and strengthening long-term national security (NAFSA, 2003; National Academies, 2005).

The intent of this chapter is to increase awareness among higher education scholars and practitioners of the policy issues affecting international students' access to America's colleges and universities and to describe the recent developments and changes in policy and regulations that are relevant to international education. This chapter is organized in five sections. First, the changes in international student enrollment as well as their characteristics, such as nationality, area of study, and financial source, are presented. Second, the implementation of SEVIS in 2003 and its implications for international education in U.S. higher education are discussed. The third section identifies the challenges for student services on campuses to providing a welcoming academic environment for international students and scholars. The fourth section addresses learning opportunities for American students to enhance their understanding of world affairs and globalization. The last section concludes this chapter with recommendations for student services practitioners and researchers in higher education to enhance international education in U.S. institutions of higher education.

Changes in International Student Enrollment

During the last half century, as Table 5.1 shows, the number of international students enrolled in America's higher education institutions steadily increased until the 2003–04 academic year. That year saw the first decline of international student enrollment since 1949, by 2.4 percent (Chin and Gallup-Black, 2004). Although the number of students from India continues to increase and India remains foremost among places of origin of international students, most Asian countries sent fewer students to U.S. colleges and universities in 2003–04 than in the previous years. According to these figures from the Institute for International Education (IIE), the number of international students whose places of origin are the leading four countries—India, China, Republic of Korea, and Japan—accounts for 41 percent of all international students enrolled during the 2003–04 academic year. Among the countries in Asia, the number of students from Japan, Thailand, and Indonesia has decreased by 11.2 percent, 10.5 percent, and 14.9 percent, respectively. Such a sharp decline in the number of Asian students contributed to the decline in enrollment in intensive English programs (14.8 percent) as well as in mathematics and computer science majors (5.9 percent). For many Asian students, intensive English programs are the entry point of their academic experience in the United States.

International educators argue that the recent economic turmoil in Asia and the difficulty of obtaining student visas from the United States were major causes of the enrollment decrease (Desruisseax, 1999; McMurtrie, 2001; Mooney and Neelakantan, 2004). Approximately 67 percent of international students report that their primary source of funds to pay for their education come from personal and family resources (Chin and Gallup-Black, 2004). With the recent tuition hikes in the United States, international students find attractive educational opportunities in other countries, such as Australia, Britain, and Canada, to maximize their financial resources (McMurtrie, 2001; Mooney and Neelakantan, 2004). In addition to financial reasons, many international educators agree that the changes in immigration policy and regulations in the United States after the terrorists' attack on September 11, 2001, have affected the enrollment of international students (Kless, 2004; Mooney and Neelakantan, 2004).

Table 5.1. International Student Enrollment in the United States: 2001–2004.

Rank in 2003–04	Place of Origin	2001–02	Annual % change	2002–03	Annual % change	2003–04	Annual % change
1	India	66,836	22.3	74,603	11.6	79,736	6.9
2	China	63,211	5.5	64,757	2.4	61,765	−4.6
3	Republic of Korea	49,046	7.4	51,519	5.0	52,484	1.9
4	Japan	46,810	0.7	45,960	−1.8	40,835	−11.2
5	Canada	26,514	4.9	26,513	0.0	27,017	1.9
6	Taiwan	28,930	1.3	28,017	−3.2	26,178	-6.6
7	Mexico	12,518	17.3	12,801	2.3	13,329	4.1
8	Turkey	12,091	10.1	11,601	−4.1	11,398	−1.7
9	Thailand	11,606	3.7	9,982	−14.0	8,937	−10.5
10	Indonesia	11,614	−0.1	10,432	−10.2	8,880	−14.9
	World total	582,996	6.4	586,323	0.6	572,509	−2.4

Sources: Chin, H. K. (ed.), 2002, 2003, 2004.

Impact of SEVIS on International Students

In November 2001, IIE conducted a survey to collect information from international admissions staff at postsecondary institutions in the United States. The findings revealed a higher rate of visa denials for males from Middle Eastern countries (Institute of International Education, 2001). These visa delays were evident even before the implementation of SEVIS. What makes international educators increasingly worried is that SEVIS is under the control of the Bureau of Immigration and Customs Enforcement, the law-enforcement division of the Department of Homeland Security (DHS), while all other matters relating to international students are administered by the Bureau of Citizenship and Immigration Services of DHS (Arnone, 2003a). International educators also fear that the strong emphasis on law enforcement from DHS will alienate or deter potential international students from coming to the United States. For example, international student service professionals provide additional assistance to male students from Arab and Muslim countries, so that they can comply with immigration mandates and who then could be invited by federal officials for photographing, fingerprinting, and interviews (Kless, 2004).

The scrutiny of the security clearance and visa regulations also creates hurdles for international students who leave the United States temporarily. For example, for many international scholars, participation in academic and scientific exchanges at conferences and meetings overseas has been limited (Kless, 2004). In other instances, such as visiting family for holidays and participating in weddings and funerals, international students have to clear every detail of the immigration requirements for their re-entry to the United States.

Transition in Student Services and Support

When international student service professionals prepared for the SEVIS data submission deadline in August 2003, many of them closed their doors to students (Arnone, 2003b). Federal agencies, such as the Department of Homeland Security, the Federal Bureau of Investigation, and the Internal Revenue Service, do not allow even a microscopic human error in SEVIS data reporting. Pressures for protecting current international students from noncompliant status that could result in denial of a visa renewal, re-entry, or deportation only have intensified in the past two years (Kless, 2004).

Though the workload of the international student service professionals significantly increased in order to comply with the new federal policy and regulations, many did not receive additional human resources. The result is less face-to-face time for current international students on campus and less time for recruiting potential students. Furthermore, it has become increasingly difficult for international student service professionals to serve as counselors, advisers, and advocates in a stringent law-enforcement environment

NEW DIRECTIONS FOR STUDENT SERVICES • DOI: 10.1002/ss

(Kless, 2004). International student service professionals have also recognized that additional efforts are required to reverse the negative perceptions toward access to American higher education among prospective and current international students (Bollag, 2004). The success of other countries, such as Australia, Britain, Canada, and New Zealand, in recruiting international students appears to result from their active interaction with potential international students in their recruitment efforts (Kless, 2004; Mooney and Neelakantan, 2004; McMurtrie, 2005). Finding more appealing educational environments, such as less expensive cost of study, less time to obtain a degree, and less restrictive work regulations, in these countries, international students are turning away from educational opportunities in the United States (Mooney and Neelakantan, 2004). The globalization of the world economy adds another dimension to this competition. China, for instance, encourages students to stay in the country to facilitate promotion of their higher education systems (McMurtrie, 2005) and their global economic development. From the compliance and enforcement of SEVIS data reporting to the demands for international student recruitment, the role of international student service professionals has changed dramatically during the last few years.

How can colleges and universities in the United States alleviate the negative perceptions toward the recent changes in immigration policies among international students? To what extent do international education services and programs continue to evolve and advocate for contributions of international education to maintain our national security and develop global understanding? These questions are addressed in the next section.

Student Services and Support Programs for Global Understanding

To alleviate the negative perceptions among international students, international student service professionals are aware of the need to provide services for both international students and American students. Specifically, a critical role of programs and services for American students to enhance their understanding of world affairs and globalization has been recognized by international educators and leaders in colleges and universities in the past several years. In 2000, the U.S. Department of State and the U.S. Department of Education founded International Education Week (IEW) in the month of November "to promote programs that prepare Americans for a global environment and attract future leaders from abroad to study, learn, and exchange experiences in the United States" (U.S. Department of State and U.S. Department of Education, 2005). During International Education Week, colleges and universities highlight the significance of international education and exchange through various programs. Some of the recommended activities by the government sponsors of IEW include hosting an International Career Day by inviting alumni or local international experts as speakers; producing a video about the experiences of international students on your campus and students back from a semester or year abroad; organizing a festival spotlighting a particular country or region; and participating in a Model UN or playing host to a high school Model UN (U.S. Department of State and U.S. Department of Education, 2005). Development and implementation of programs that facilitate collaboration among international education service professionals and faculty are also encouraged for IEW activities. For example, faculty who conducted research abroad or served as a Fulbright scholar can be invited to a panel discussion or symposium to address the importance of international exchanges. International education service professionals and faculty can also provide vital learning opportunities for students in classrooms by inviting other professionals with overseas experiences, such as former diplomats, Peace Corps volunteers, journalists, or global business leaders, to talk about international careers, the importance of foreign language study and study abroad opportunities, and international and intercultural communication (U.S. Department of State and U.S. Department of Education, 2005).

Strengthen partnerships with faculty through study abroad programs. It is noteworthy that partnerships among international education service professionals and faculty have long been established through offering study abroad programs in American colleges and universities. A body of research has documented the benefits American students receive from their unique learning experiences with study abroad programs (Douglas and Jones-Rikkers, 2001; Kiely and Nielson, 2003; Peterson and others, 1999; Sowa, 2002). Although participation of American students in study abroad programs increased by 129 percent during the last decade, Western European and Latin American countries have been continuously chosen as the leading destinations for study abroad (Chin and Gallup-Black, 2004). Spanish and other major languages of Western Europe are popular choices of study among American students enrolled in foreign-language courses (Cummings, 2001). Only a small number of students enroll in courses in languages of Asian countries and Middle Eastern countries—6 percent and 2 percent, respectively (Cummings, 2001). To facilitate the enhancement of global understanding, this imbalance in regional coverage by study abroad programs and foreign-language courses should be improved. Study abroad programs in non-English-speaking countries, such as African, Middle Eastern, and South Asian countries, should be promoted to provide valuable learning opportunities for American students to experience and understand diverse cultures, religious beliefs, and languages.

Strengthen partnerships with students. There is no doubt that exposing oneself to a foreign environment can offer the best opportunity for learning another language and culture. However, there are numerous ways that international education service professionals can provide American students with learning about diverse cultures and foreign languages and help them understand globalization. For instance, international education service professionals can create an online chat room or an informal orientation

NEW DIRECTIONS FOR STUDENT SERVICES • DOI: 10.1002/ss

program on their Web site for prospective international students; such services could be hosted by American students who could help international students learn about the host institution and its surrounding environment. Furthermore, international education service professionals can establish consortiums among international student organizations and American student organizations to promote intra-organizational communication within an institution. A consortium can be founded based on a particular interest among diverse student organizations, such as arts, music, and business, taking them beyond their cultural boundaries.

Conclusions and Implications for Practice

The changes in federal regulations and policies during the past four years have required international student service professionals to adopt numerous new responsibilities while maintaining their excellence in creating a diverse and global campus. Recovery from the recent declining trend of international student enrollment and the negative perceptions of American institutions of higher education may take several years. A more cohesive approach to recruitment, which includes legal and regulatory issues, financial issues, and marketing strategy, is critical to attracting international students and scholars to the United States.

A plethora of recommendations for international student service professionals have addressed the issue of internationalizing the campus (Carmical, 2002; Christie and Ragans, 1999; Ping, 1999) as well as providing academic and social services to international students (Abel, 2002; Lacina, 2002; Murphy, Hawkes, and Law, 2002; Peterson and others, 1999). Although many of these recommendations are relevant, the following recommendations are created specifically for divisions of student affairs and international student service professionals to address recent and future challenges. As federal mandates increase, institutions of higher education need to recognize the multidimensional aspects of international student service professionals. It is critical that these professionals receive continuing professional development training. Further, it is recommended that divisions of student affairs conduct a needs assessment that measures competencies in processing the data in SEVIS as well as the staff member's familiarity with changes in laws and regulations for international student service professionals. Even while demands for compliance of federal regulations continue to increase, international student service professionals should still be able to create welcoming support for students and scholars. Further, international student service professionals should survey international students and scholars to encourage them to express their reasons for visiting their campuses. Their responses on the application process as well as admission experiences can provide important information for international student service professionals. The information can be used to develop services and programs to better serve these students and their transition to college. As a collective effort, international student service professionals can implement a multi-institutional study to identify barriers and areas of improvements for SEVIS and other policy issues. Innovative approaches to international student recruitment also can be facilitated. For instance, a comprehensive institutional recruitment plan that includes establishing and maintaining frequent communication with prospective students via e-mail messages, mailing a complete and detailed admission package and newsletters to prospective students, and providing a personalized Web site to track students' application status can be developed and implemented to create a welcoming image of an institution (McMurtrie, 2005). American universities and colleges also can develop academic transfer programs with institutions in other nations. International students can begin their studies in their home countries and complete their studies through a transfer process at a partner institution in the United States (McMurtrie, 2005).

Intensity of the threat of global terrorism should not compromise the contributions of international students and scholars to the nation's academic and scientific advancement and economic prosperity. The enhancement of international education in United States higher education can be promoted while maintaining our national security.

References

Abel, C. F. "Academic Success and the International Student: Research and Recommendations." In B. W. Speck and B. H. Carmical (eds.), *Internationalizing Higher Education: Building Vital Programs on Campuses.* New Directions for Higher Education, no. 117. San Francisco: Jossey-Bass, 2002.

Arnone, M. "Reorganization of U.S. Agencies Leaves Colleges Worried About How Foreign Students Will Be Treated." *Chronicle of Higher Education,* Mar. 7, 2003a, p. A28.

Arnone, M. "Colliding Deadlines May Create a 'Perfect Storm' for International-Student Offices." *Chronicle of Higher Education,* Aug. 1, 2003b, p. A21.

Bollag, B. "Enrollment of Foreign Students Drops in the U.S." *Chronicle of Higher Education,* Nov. 19, 2004, p. A1.

Carmical, B. H. "Internationalizing the Campus: What Do You Need to Know?" In B. W. Speck and B. H. Carmical (eds.), *Internationalizing Higher Education: Building Vital Programs on Campuses.* New Directions for Higher Education, no. 117. San Francisco: Jossey-Bass, 2002.

Chin, H. K. (ed.). *Open Doors 2002: Report on International Educational Exchange.* New York: Institute on International Education, 2002.

Chin, H. K. (ed.). *Open Doors 2003: Report on International Educational Exchange.* New York: Institute on International Education, 2003.

Chin, H. K., and Gallup-Black, A. (eds.). *Open Doors 2004: Report on International Educational Exchange.* New York: Institute on International Education, 2004.

Christie, R. A., and Ragans, S. W. "Beyond Borders: A Model for Student and Staff Development." In J. W. Curtis (ed.), *Beyond Borders: How International Developments Are Changing Student Affairs Practice.* New Directions for Student Services, no. 86. San Francisco: Jossey-Bass, 1999.

Cummings, W. "Current Challenges of International Education." *ERIC Digest, 2001.* http://wdcrobcolp01.ed.gov/CFAPPS/ERIC/resumes/records.cfm?ericnum=ED464523. Accessed Oct. 16, 2005.

Desruisseax, P. "Foreign Students Continue to Flock to the U.S." *Chronicle of Higher Education*, Dec. 10, 1999, p. A57.

Douglas, C., and Jones-Rikkers, C. G. "Study Abroad Programs in American Student Worldmindedness: An Empirical Analysis." *Journal of Teaching in International Business*, 2001, *13*(1), 55–66.

Institute of International Education. "Summary of the Post September 11 International Admissions Communications Survey," 2001. http://opendoors.iienetwork. org/?p=29117. Accessed Aug. 13, 2005.

Kiely, R., and Nielson, D. "International Service Learning: The Importance of Partnerships." *Community College Journal*, Jan. 2003, 39–41.

Kless, S. H. "We Threaten National Security by Discouraging the Best and Brightest Students from Abroad." *Chronicle of Higher Education*, Oct. 4, 2004, p. B9.

Lacina, J. G. "Preparing International Students for a Successful Social Experience in Higher Education." In B. W. Speck and B. H. Carmical (eds.), *Internationalizing Higher Education: Building Vital Programs on Campuses.* New Directions for Higher Education, no. 117. San Francisco: Jossey-Bass, 2002.

McMurtrie, B. "Foreign Enrollments Grow in the U.S., but So Does Competition from Other Nations." *Chronicle of Higher Education*, Nov. 16, 2001, pp. A45–A47.

McMurtrie, B. "American Universities Step Up Their Sales Pitch Overseas." *Chronicle of Higher Education*, Feb. 11, 2005, p. A8.

Mooney, P., and Neelakantan, S. "No Longer Dreaming of America." *Chronicle of Higher Education*, Oct. 8, 2004, p. A41.

Murphy, C., Hawkes, L., and Law, J. "How International Students Can Benefit from a Web-Based College Orientation." In B. W. Speck and B. H. Carmical (eds.), *Internationalizing Higher Education: Building Vital Programs on Campuses.* New Directions for Higher Education, no. 117. San Francisco: Jossey-Bass, 2002.

NAFSA Association of International Educators. "Strategic Task Force on International Student Access." In *America's Interest: Welcoming International Students*, 2003. Washington, D.C.: NAFSA Association of International Educators, 2003.

National Academies. "Recommendations for Enhancing the U.S. Visa System to Advance America's Scientific and Economic Competitiveness and National Security Interests," 2005. http://www4.nationalacademies.org/news.nsf/isbn/s05182005?Open. Accessed Aug. 13, 2005.

Peterson, D. M., and others. "Contributions of International Students and Programs to Campus Diversity." In J. W. Curtis (ed.), *Beyond Borders: How International Developments Are Changing Student Affairs Practice.* New Directions for Student Services, no. 86. San Francisco: Jossey-Bass, 1999.

Ping, C. J. "An Expanded International Role for Student Affairs." In J. W. Curtis (ed.), *Beyond Borders: How International Developments Are Changing Student Affairs Practice.* New Directions for Student Services, no. 86. San Francisco: Jossey-Bass, 1999.

Sowa, P. A. "How Valuable Are Student Exchange Programs?" In B. W. Speck and B. H. Carmical (eds.), *Internationalizing Higher Education: Building Vital Programs on Campuses.* New Directions for Higher Education, no. 117. San Francisco: Jossey-Bass, 2002.

U.S. Department of State and U.S. Department of Education. "International Week 2005," 2005. http://iew.state.gov/. Accessed Oct. 14, 2005.

SOKO S. STAROBIN is a postdoctoral research associate in the department of educational leadership and policy studies at Iowa State University in Ames, Iowa.

NEW DIRECTIONS FOR STUDENT SERVICES • DOI: 10.1002/ss

6

This chapter discusses the challenges, characteristics, and transitional roles of adult learners. Implications for student services professionals are presented.

Adult Learners in Transition

Jonathan I. Compton, Elizabeth Cox,
Frankie Santos Laanan

Adult learners are a rapidly growing segment of the postsecondary student population. While many in student services use the terms *nontraditional* and *adult student* interchangeably, we argue that adult students have particular characteristics that set them apart from nontraditional students. In order to understand who these students are it is necessary to clear up some of the confusion about the difference between adult students and nontraditional students. A century ago, nontraditional students would have been identified by race, gender, or socioeconomic status (Ogren, 2003). More recently, that definition was simplified to nontraditional students being those age twenty-five or older. Today, the definition has expanded. Now nontraditional students are those who have at least one of the following characteristics: they delay postsecondary enrollment one year or more after high school graduation, enroll part time, are employed full time, are financially independent of their parents, have dependents other than a spouse, are single parents, or do not have a high school diploma (National Center for Education Statistics, 2002). According to the National Center for Education Statistics (NCES, 2002), 73 percent of all undergraduates are nontraditional in some way, making them the majority rather than the exception on today's campuses.

Adult students are often referred to as nontraditional students, yet not all nontraditional students are adult students. Despite some overlap between the definition of nontraditional students and adult students (for example, adult students are also age twenty-five years and over), there are characteristics of

NEW DIRECTIONS FOR STUDENT SERVICES, no. 114, Summer 2006 © Wiley Periodicals, Inc.
Published online in Wiley InterScience (www.interscience.wiley.com) • DOI: 10.1002/ss.208

adult students that deserve our attention and the recognition that these students are a distinct group. First, adult students are more likely to be pursuing a program leading to a vocational certificate or degree. As a result, many choose to enroll in community colleges. Second, adult students have focused goals for their education, typically to gain or enhance work skills. Many adult students view education as a means of transporting themselves from one phase of life to another (Aslanian, 2001). A third characteristic of adult learners is that they consider themselves primarily workers and not students. With all of the other outside obligations in an adult learner's life, being a student very well may be a lower priority than being a spouse and father or mother, too. A fourth characteristic is that adult students are more likely to be enrolled in distance education. Again, with all of their other responsibilities, adult students are seeking education that can fit into their busy lives; distance education is a means to make that happen. In 2005, NCES found that adult learners also were more likely to speak a language other than English. This fifth factor indicates that adult learners may have an additional hurdle to cross before even enrolling in basic collegiate coursework. And finally, a report published by NCES (2002) found that adult learners are more likely to leave postsecondary education without earning a degree.

Increase of Nontraditional and Adult Student Enrollment

Several factors have led to the increasing number of adult and nontraditional students on our campuses and in our classrooms. According to the 2000 Census, of the 182 million individuals age twenty-five and older, 126 million have not completed an educational degree beyond a high school diploma (U.S. Bureau of the Census, 2000). In addition, for many regions of the United States, the numbers of high school graduates will continue to decrease for the foreseeable future, so adult students are a market to be tapped. A second factor is the decline of the blue-collar sector of the economy. Outsourcing and layoffs have forced many adults back into the labor pool only to find they no longer have the necessary skills to become gainfully employed. Thus, more adults are going back to school to increase their work skills or to learn new skills as the new economy is filled with positions that require workers with a more technologically sophisticated skill set. The final factor, the changing norms in society, is perhaps the single most important contributor for the number of adult women who have enrolled in postsecondary education. No longer is it the norm for women to stay in the home and be full-time mothers and housewives—many families would not be able to support that notion economically even if they wanted to. Today, women are the majority population in postsecondary education.

The majority of adult students are led back to higher education due to a major life transition, such as divorce, widowhood, or career change. Each of these factors constitutes a huge change in an individual's life. Now added to that is the additional transition and pressure of enrolling in postsecondary education.

Current Literature

Research on nontraditional students and adult students often does not differentiate between the two groups of students. Current literature regarding nontraditional students focuses on how best to address the needs of the so-called underserved (Ogren, 2003). Considering the factors listed above, this is not necessarily an accurate portrayal of adult students' needs or what they bring to higher education. This view is based on a deficit model that implies that adult students are not prepared for higher education. Institutions tend to focus on the obstacles adult students face when returning to school (such as finances, family obligations, and time constraints), as they have a direct impact on the one role the institution recognizes for the adult learner, that of student. Some scholars would argue that adult learners are actually more capable of learning than their younger counterparts because of their ability to use their prior experiences in order to process new ideas and situations and that the obstacles faced could actually be seen as strengths for adult learners (Richardson and King, 1998).

Student services professionals need to be cognizant of the tendency to treat adult students as one type of nontraditional students or as a homogeneous group. Along with the factors listed above, adult students tend to be more diverse than their traditional-aged counterparts in their expectations of an institution, their motivation for attending college, and their experiences with higher education (Richardson and King, 1998). Given these insights, coupled with the fact that the numbers of adult learners will continue to increase, student services professionals must adjust to serve this population more effectively. As Aslanian (2001) stated, "Adults in America today—and even more so in the future—cannot stop learning. They will be back, over and over, throughout their lifetimes" (p. 58). Our adult learners will experience transition again and again.

Adult Learning-Focused Institutions

It is worthwhile to examine what some exemplary institutions are doing to serve adult learners. The Council for Adult and Experiential Learning (CAEL) is a nonprofit organization whose mission is to provide institutions of higher education and other stakeholders with "the tools and strategies they need for creating practical, effective lifelong learning solutions" (CAEL, 2005). They have developed a framework and assessment tool for institutions to evaluate effectiveness in serving adult learners. Their initial eight principles of effective service to adult learners are shown in Exhibit 6.1.

Exhibit 6.1. Eight Principles of Effectiveness for Serving Adult Learners.

• *Outreach.* The institution conducts outreach to adult learners by overcoming barriers of time, place, and tradition in order to create lifelong access to educational opportunities.

• *Life and career planning.* The institution addresses adult learners' life and career goals before or at the onset of enrollment in order to assess and align its capacities to help learners reach their goals.

• *Financing.* The institution uses an array of payment options for adult learners in order to expand equity and financial flexibility.

• *Assessment of learning outcomes.* The institution defines and assesses the knowledge, skills, and competencies acquired by adult learners both from the curriculum and from life-work experience in order to assign credit and confer degrees with rigor.

• *Teaching-learning process.* The institution's faculty uses multiple methods of instruction (including experiential- and problem-based methods) for adult learners in order to connect curricular concepts to useful knowledge and skills.

• *Student support systems.* The institution assists adult learners using comprehensive academic and student support systems in order to enhance students' capacities to become self-directed, lifelong learners.

• *Technology.* The institution uses information technology to provide relevant and timely information to enhance the learning experience.

• *Strategic partnerships.* The institution engages in strategic relationships, partnerships, and collaborations with employers and other organizations in order to develop and improve educational opportunities for adult learners.

Source: Council for Adult and Experiential Learning, 2005.

Using this framework, CAEL has identified the following six institutions that they consider to exhibit best practices in the area of service to adult students:

Athabasca University in Athabasca, Alberta, Canada (four-year, public)
Empire State College in Saratoga Springs, New York (four-year, public)
Marylhurst University in Marylhurst, Oregon (four-year, private)
School of New Resources at the College of New Rochelle in New Rochelle, New York (four-year, public)
School for New Learning at DePaul University in Chicago, Illinois (four-year, public)
Sinclair Community College in Dayton, Ohio (two-year, public)

Several themes emerge from analyzing the approaches that these institutions take.

Validating Experiential Learning. First, all six of these institutions place a value on experiential learning. Adult learners bring a wealth of life and work experience with them when they enter higher education. All of these institutions offer credit for this experience, either through testing or through a portfolio system. Marylhurst University in Oregon, for example, uses a portfolio system for students to document their prior learning. The students participate in a learning assessment workshop and work with a prior learning assessment advisor, who helps each student develop a portfolio. The process may be done in either a traditional or online format, and students may be eligible for up to forty-five "quarter credits" for life and work experience (Marylhurst University, 2005).

The School for New Learning at DePaul University observes that the value of recognizing experiential learning is that it validates what students already know and helps the learner to accelerate their program of study: "SNL believes that it matters more what you know than where you've learned that skill. So, we invite you to present evidence of what you already know, so you can use your time in college on 'new learning' rather than repeat what you already know. . . . . Experience is powerful, and . . . . education is most effective if you leave a class able to apply what you learned to a new situation or problem. So we value the experience you have already had and include hands-on activities in classes and projects, encouraging experimentation and risk-taking" (DePaul University, 2005).

Customized Educational Plan. In addition to offering credit for experiential learning, each of these institutions provides some form of a customized educational plan. For example, the School of New Resources at the College of New Rochelle provides a variety of options, such as seminars and independent study, for students to pursue subjects that are relevant to them in ways that are most suitable to them. Students are encouraged to collaborate with faculty to develop alternative independent study opportunities, such as research projects, internships, or telecourses. These forms of study provide new and engaging learning opportunities that are customized to the needs and interests of individual students (College of New Rochelle, 2005).

Sinclair Community College in Dayton, Ohio, has a program called College Without Walls. In this program, each student works with one faculty advisor (called the Core Faculty) to create a learning contract for each course. The learning contract is "a comprehensive guide for achieving course objectives and evaluation of the work." It outlines the objectives of the course, the responsibilities of the student, how the work will be evaluated, and the timeframe in which the student will complete the coursework. The document is signed by the student, the instructor, and the advisor. This approach allows for a flexible time limit for students who need to work at their own pace, on their own time, and from any location, with minimal reliance on technology (Sinclair Community College, 2005).

Support for Distance Learning. All of these institutions provide some form of distance learning. Athabasca University in Alberta, Canada, is an open university specializing primarily in distance learning for adults. Located in a relatively sparsely populated region, the university provides services such as sending library books to students through the mail to overcome geographic barriers. Also, because distance courses can be isolating, each student in the university is assigned a campus-based tutor whom students may contact as needed for support (Athabasca University, 2005).

The university provides individualized study courses and grouped-study or online courses. Individualized study courses provide students with materials and resources as well as an on-campus tutor whom they may contact as needed. Students are responsible to work through the material at their own pace. Many of the classes provided by Athabasca do not have an enrollment deadline. This is helpful for adult learners, because transitions such as losing a job can happen at any time (Athabasca University, 2005).

Student Support and Student Services. Empire State College in New York is a leader in adult learning and part of the State University of New York (SUNY) system that specializes in educating adults. One way in which the college provides support for students is through its library. The library provides many online resources as well as access to libraries at any SUNY institution. Other online resources, such as an online mathematics library and an online writing resource center, are available to both on-campus and distance students at all hours (Empire State, 2005).

While these online support systems are useful and valuable, it is also essential that students are able to make contact with a tutor, mentor, advisor, or faculty member when they need to talk to a real person. At Empire State College, each student is assigned a faculty mentor who works with the student to develop a tailored degree program that is relevant to the needs of the student and who assists and encourages the student in achieving his or her goals (Empire State, 2005).

An overarching theme for all of these CAEL institutions is flexibility and creativity. Institutions that serve adult students must be willing to be flexible to serve them in perhaps unconventional ways. It is well known that adult students need flexibility in terms of time and location, but they also need flexibility in other ways as well. Flexibility includes allowing adults to work with faculty advisors to customize their program of study according to their goals.

Implications for Student Affairs Professionals

Adult students continually make transitions—from employee to parent to student and back again. Student affairs professionals need to be cognizant of this transitioning and acknowledge and support the larger context of adult learners' lives and the demands placed on them. A goal of education should be to help develop the whole person, not just a single facet of an individual.

If we as student affairs professionals and educators are truly interested in creating a student-centered environment, many factors must be considered. As has been demonstrated, adult learners have many competing interests for their time, attention, and energy, all of which may cause a great deal of stress. However, stress properly funneled can be a positive factor.

Programs that wish to serve adult learners effectively should reconsider traditional practices in order to accommodate these learners. First, they should reduce the time and effort necessary for adult learners to move through the system. This may include validation of experiential learning from life and work experience.

Second, institutional leaders should review the institution's instructional delivery system to consider whether courses are offered in a variety of formats and whether students have a choice of instructors. Instructors, advisors, and support services must also be accessible when students need them.

Third, coursework should have practical applications. Adults tend to have career-focused goals, and they will often value courses and assignments that are seen as relevant to their goals. For example, instructors could allow projects completed in the workplace to count for credit, or they could make workplace-related assignments.

Fourth, adult students should be encouraged to be more integrated into the social life of the institution. Research shows that the greater the social integration the more likely a student will continue enrollment (Community College Survey of Student Engagement, 2004). Such integration presents a challenge, since adult learners tend to see their support and social networks as being external to the institution; consequently, they are not highly interested in social activities and being involved in the life of the institution. Institutions should seek out creative ways to make these students feel more involved and engaged in the institution.

Fifth, counseling centers should be available to help students cope with emotional, physical, intellectual, cultural, vocational, relational, and other transitions (Haggan, 2000). Such centers should offer programs or workshops on stress in order to help students understand their stress and deal with it appropriately.

Finally, our institutions need to take a proactive approach to uncovering the needs of adult learners, rather than waiting until the traditional exit interview or "autopsy study" to learn about problems (Bean and Metzner, 1985). A proactive approach to serving adult learners requires flexibility, adaptability, and creativity.

References

Aslanian, C. "You're Never Too Old." *Community College Journal*, 2001, 71(5), 56–58.

Athabasca University. *About Athabasca University*, 2005. http://www.athabascau.ca/aboutAU/. Accessed Aug. 3, 2005.

Bean, J. P., and Metzner, B. S. "A Conceptual Model of Nontraditional Undergraduate Student Attrition." *Review of Educational Research*, 1985, 55(4), 485–540.

College of New Rochelle, School of New Resources. 2005. http://www.cnr.edu/ACADE-MICS/snr-index.html. Accessed Aug. 3, 2005.

Community College Survey of Student Engagement. *Engagement by Design: Summary of 2004 Findings*, 2004. http://www.ccsse.org/publications/CCSSE_reportfinal2004.pdf. Accessed Oct. 5, 2005.

Council for Adult and Experiential Learning. *Introduction to the Adult Learning Focused Institution Initiative (ALFI)*, 2005. http://www.cael.org/alfi.htm. Accessed July 20, 2005.

DePaul University, School for New Learning. *For Prospective Students,* 2005. http://www.snl.depaul.edu/prospective/undergrad_index.asp. Accessed Aug. 3, 2005.

Empire State College. *Succeed with Our Flexible Approach,* 2005. http://www.esc.edu/esconline/online2.nsf/html/ourflexibleapproach.html. Accessed Aug. 3, 2005.

Haggan, P. S. "Transition Counseling in the Community College." *Community College Journal of Research and Practice,* 2000, *24,* 427–442.

Marylhurst University. *Prior Learning Assessment,* 2005. http://www.marylhurst.edu/lac-info/index.html. Accessed Aug. 3, 2005.

National Center for Education Statistics (NCES). *Waiting to Attend College,* 2005. http://nces.ed.gov/das/epubs/2005152/. Accessed Aug. 3, 2005.

National Center for Education Statistics. *Nontraditional Undergraduates,* 2002. http://nces.ed.gov/programs/coe/2002/analyses/nontraditional/index.asp. Accessed Aug. 3, 2005.

Ogren, C. A. "Rethinking the 'Nontraditional' Student from a Historical Perspective." *Journal of Higher Education,* 2003, *74*(6), 640–664.

Richardson, J.T.E., and King, E. "Adult Students in Higher Education." *Journal of Higher Education,* 1998, *69*(1), 65–88.

Sinclair Community College. *College Without Walls,* 2005. http://www.sinclair.edu/academics/elhs/departments/ebe/cww/index.cfm. Accessed Aug. 3, 2005.

U.S. Bureau of the Census. *American Factfinder: Educational Attainment by Sex: 2000.* http://factfinder.census.gov/servlet/SAFFPeople?_sse=on. Accessed Oct. 5, 2005.

JONATHAN I. COMPTON AND ELIZABETH COX *are doctoral students and research associates in the department of educational leadership and policy studies at Iowa State University.*

FRANKIE SANTOS LAANAN *is associate professor in the department of educational leadership and policy studies at Iowa State University.*

NEW DIRECTIONS FOR STUDENT SERVICES • DOI: 10.1002/ss

The number of students of color transferring to and completing degrees at four-year, non-research-extensive universities continues to increase. However, research-extensive universities struggle with recruiting and retaining students of color. This chapter discusses one initiative developed by a research-extensive university focused on increasing success and graduation rates of students of color.

Increasing Retention and Success of Students of Color at Research-Extensive Universities

Steven R. Aragon, Mario Rios Perez

Research and funding concentrating on students of color in higher education institutions have recently remained at the forefront for foundations, scholars, and academic departments seeking to increase the representation of students of color in colleges and universities. Most studies, whether in primary, secondary, or higher education, focus on so-called proper retention of these students of color. At the height of the debate, topics varying from cultural to institutional critiques delve into this discussion. In higher education, specific discussions have surfaced regarding college access, persistence, and graduation (Cofer and Somers, 2001; Dowd, 2003). Current data show that, although many students of color are entering higher education institutions, few matriculate into research-oriented universities. Furthermore, a disappointing proportion graduate and ultimately pursue graduate or professional degrees.

Although the causal factors leading to the underrepresentation of students of color in higher education are debated hotly, national data clearly demonstrate that African American, American Indian, and Latino students

---

Note: The authors wish to thank the Center on Democracy in a Multiracial Society for providing the resources used in conducting the research upon which this chapter is based. We would also like to thank Ave Alvarado, director, and Coleman Evans, graduate assistant of the Educational Equity Programs Office, for their assistance in organizing the data collection sessions and insight into the AYRE Program.

continue to stay away from baccalaureate-granting institutions, especially those that are research extensive, and opt to enroll in America's community colleges.

As of the national 2002 fall undergraduate enrollment, students of color accounted for approximately 31 percent of all enrollment in degree-granting institutions, with African Americans representing 12 percent, Latinos 11 percent, Asians-Pacific Islanders 7 percent, and American Indians–Alaska Natives 1 percent (National Center for Education Statistics, 2004). Students of color comprised approximately 36 percent of the enrollment in public and private two-year degree-granting institutions. However, National Center for Education Statistics (NCES) data show that 48 percent of all students of color, but only 37 percent of all white students, enrolled in higher education were enrolled in two-year colleges. Similarly, 41 percent of all Asian–Pacific Islander, 43 percent of all African American, 49 percent of all American Indian–Alaska Native, and 58 percent of all Latino students in higher education were found within two-year colleges (NCES, 2004). National data show that students enrolled in community colleges usually are nontraditional when compared to students enrolled in four-year institutions. Community college students overwhelmingly are older, disproportionately students of color, employed at least part-time, attend college part-time, and enroll in remediation courses. Although not all community college students aspire to earn a baccalaureate degree, these factors prove deleterious to the smooth transfer to research-extensive institutions (Laanan, 2003; Dowd, 2003; Pascarella and Terenzini, 1991; Bettinger and Long, 2005).

Background

Community colleges are a sector of American higher education termed the *terra incognita* (Callan, 1997) because few researchers attempt to address the experiences of their students and because of the position these institutions hold in the history of American higher education (Hutcheson, 1999; Townsend, Bragg, and Kinnick, 2003). Some scholars openly neglect community colleges because they believe a "BA is the standard-bearer of the post-secondary education" (Swail, Redd, and Perna, 2003, p. 3). The large convergence of research on four-year institutions remains true, although the American Council on Education (ACE) found that in 1999–2000 42 percent of students enrolled in higher education institutions attended a community college (2002).

Data show that African American, American Indian, and Latino students are more likely to attend a public two-year institution. Swail, Redd, and Perna (2003) assert that the neglect of community college students may be "problematic for [institutions] interested in increasing bachelor degree completion rates of transfer from public two-year colleges to four-year institutions" (p. 18). The lack of attention four-year institutions give to community colleges proves counterproductive when they seek to increase the number of students of color in four-year institutions.

NEW DIRECTIONS FOR STUDENT SERVICES • DOI: 10.1002/ss

The first impulse of researchers is to examine how the community college fosters the transfer process; consequently, they overlook a vital facet of the transfer process—that is, the pivotal role four-year institutions play in the recruitment, transition, retention, and eventual graduation of these students. Deepening this research dilemma is the lack of research on how four-year university programs facilitate the transfer function for community college students.

Though the efforts engaged in by community colleges are fundamental to the transfer function, in this chapter we examine the other half of the transfer process—that is, what is being done by four-year, research-extensive institutions to increase the number of students of color transferring in from community colleges. The American Association of Community Colleges (AACC) and the American Association of State Colleges and Universities (AASCU) assert this claim in a 2004 published report. AACC found they could not "hope to realize universal access to postsecondary learning without the purposeful engagement of educators at all levels" (AACC, pg. v). Current research shows that most studies have not yet focused on how research-extensive universities respond to students of color transferring from community colleges.

Overview of Barriers to Transfer

Research pertinent to the transfer process of individuals has examined how state and federal policy, college system governance, funding, and university administrators best facilitate the systematic transfer of information to students anticipating to transfer from a community college to four-year universities. As Welsh (2002) demonstrates, many states confront information barriers to interinstitutional transfer students that preclude a smooth transition from one university system to another. Welsh's study examines the effectiveness of state information systems in collecting information that improves the interchange of student information between institutions. According to Welsh, the prime interest of many senior academic officers in developing such information infrastructures is to track students transferring from two-year institutions to a baccalaureate-granting institution. Welsh states that institutions "most likely to collect and use data to improve educational outcomes for transfer students are those that collect data on a continuous basis, collect unit records on students and have the capacity to track students from institution to institution" (p. 263). However, the study demonstrates that most higher education institutions collecting these data limit the use of this information solely to enrollment management and not for the improvement of learning outcomes.

In 2002, the American Council on Education (ACE) and the Center for Policy Analysis (CPA) released results from a ten-year longitudinal study delineating the central tenets of college access and persistence. The ACE report found students who enroll initially in community colleges commonly represent the first generation in their family to attend college and that they work part-time, increasing the risk of dropping out of college. Other studies demonstrate that the rate of educational attainment for African Americans, Latinos, and American Indians does not correspond to their demographic percentage across the country (Solórzano, Rivas, and Velez, 2005). Furthermore, data from 1995–96 show that although 48.1 percent of white students and 57.5 percent of Asian students who first enrolled in a public four-year institution earned a bachelor's degree within six years, this was not the case for other groups. For African Americans, the national percentage was 33.6 and for Latinos, 34.1 (Swail, Redd, and Perna, 2003).

Systematic and structural explanations of what impairs the transfer process vary; they include the lack of articulation agreements between institutions, ineffective information systems and databases, financial aid limitations, and unsupportive transfer policies. The most common type of articulation agreements are between community colleges and universities. That is, these agreements outline which community college courses are accepted by the universities (Cohen and Brawer, 2003). Other theoretical frameworks fault the institutional social environment as unfavorable to the transfer function. These target the cultural and institutional support that sustains the living and learning communities on college campuses (Ahumada, 1993; Brint, 2003; Ornelas and Solórzano, 2004; St. John and Starkey, 1994; Townsend and Ignash, 2000; Welsh and Kjorlien, 2001).

Transfer Shock. The transfer shock phenomenon has been examined widely to gauge the impact on community college students of transferring to a four-year institution (Carlan and Byxbe, 2000; Laanan, 2001). *Transfer shock* refers to the effect the transfer process has on the academic performance of students. Glass and Harrington (2002) examined how well community college students performed once they entered a four-year institution by comparing the GPA, retention, and graduation rates between transfer and native students. They found that students who transferred from community colleges "do as well, and, on occasion, better than native students" (p. 425). In their final assessment, they assert that community college transfer students are just as likely to graduate as their native-student counterparts. They suggest that four-year institutions should "deliberately seek out community college transfer students and make them aware of the availability of these opportunities" (p. 427).

Transfer shock has been found not to affect all entering community college students in the same manner. Students in disciplines such as the fine arts, humanities, and social sciences tend to experience an increase in their GPA, as opposed to those in mathematics or science (Cejda, 1997). Laanan (1996, 2004) further examines the transfer shock phenomenon by including the psychosocial experiences of transfer students at four-year institutions. Laanan argues that solely understanding the academic performance of transfer students is not telling of the complex factors affecting each transfer student once they enter a four-year university. As a result, many universities have responded to transfer shock by establishing programs designed to reduce the effects. For those students who do experience a drop in GPA as a result of transferring, student success courses have been developed by both

NEW DIRECTIONS FOR STUDENT SERVICES • DOI: 10.1002/ss

four-year institutions and community colleges. Such courses have proven especially beneficial for students of color enrolled in predominantly white institutions (Stovall, 2000). However, these programs are rarely established for community college students once they transfer to a four-year institution.

Overview of the Transfer Process: Community Colleges and Four-Year Universities. What remains problematic is the unwarranted emphasis given to community colleges in the transfer process. As shown by Bryant (2001), most studies examining the transfer process only focus on the contributing factors employed by community colleges in the transfer function that may lead to the student's success or failure. This establishes a constricted approach to the transfer process—-the weight continually remains on the shoulders of community colleges. Receiving institutions have ignored their role and responsibility in recruiting students of color from community colleges. If restored, this may result in higher transfer rates and an increase in the graduation rates of students of color in research-extensive universities.

Student retention models varying from Tinto to Rendón rely on the present institutional setting of the student, yet neglect students who move from one institutional structure to another. In this analysis, students transferring to four-year institutions automatically are classified as four-year students and systematically stripped of their relationship to their near past. Rendón, Jalomo, and Nora (2000) argue that Tinto's linear student retention model, which derives from Van Gennep's three major stages, inadequately depicts the experience of students of color. According to Van Gennep's model, students must first separate from where they originated, then make a transition to the new environment where new relationships are established, and finally become incorporated into "new patterns of interaction with members of the new group" (Rendón, Jalomo, and Nora, 2000, p. 132). Rendón, Jalomo, and Nora propose that these retention and persistence models are detrimental to understanding the experiences of students of color. Rather than accounting for the "bi-culturalism" or "dual socialization" of the students, a linear approach reifies a dominant culture that all students must conform to.

Overview of Recruiting Transfer Students from Community Colleges. Most prominent in the recruitment process of community college transfer students are professional schools and academic departments. For example, the School of Education at New York University (NYU) is making many strides to increase its number of transfer students. NYU has taken a proactive strategy by collaborating in establishing articulation agreements with surrounding community colleges (Wright and Middleberg, 1998). The objective is to facilitate the transfer process and enhance student retention in a number of ways: by using articulation agreements that minimize credit loss, by offering scholarship assistance to help overcome financial need, and by providing a centralized source of information and guidance to students from the time of their community college studies through their transition to NYU and until they graduate from the university.

NEW DIRECTIONS FOR STUDENT SERVICES • DOI: 10.1002/ss

With support of their surrounding community colleges and NYU's central admissions office, the School of Education established the Community College Transfer Opportunity Program (CCTOP), which facilitates the recruitment and retention of community college students. Data show that between 1990 and 1998 approximately 45 percent of approximately 550 students who transferred as a result of this program were students of color. Furthermore, 86 percent of transfer students who initially enrolled in NYU at least full-time earned a baccalaureate degree.

Similar recruitment programs have been initiated in California, where a shortage of "highly qualified" teachers, as defined by the No Child Left Behind Act of 2002, remains at the center of discussions. With this shortage and the added pressures of high teacher attrition, a retiring workforce, and an interest in diversifying the teaching profession, community colleges across the country have drawn the attention of university teacher training programs as ideal recruitment sites. The American Association of Colleges for Teacher Education (AACTE) has called for an urgent collaboration between community colleges and four-year institutions (AACTE, 2002). AACTE recognized the lack of attention given to community colleges which, in many cases, already incorporate teacher training courses that schools of education offer. Instead of exclusively fostering relationships with high schools, the community colleges now officially became "alternative providers" for four-year universities.

Community colleges are perceived as a possible resource where future teachers from diverse backgrounds can be trained to satisfy the needs of school districts. Hagedorn, Newman, and Duffy (2003) show that the recruitment of future teachers in California's community colleges was sponsored by the governor when he established the Raising Expectations, Achievement, and Development in Schools (READ) initiative, which allotted approximately $10 million for partnerships for teacher education programs between California State University (CSU) campuses and community colleges. A program established at Cerritos College in Norwalk, California, guaranteed students a slot in the CSU–Long Beach Integrated Teacher Education Program after they were admitted to the Teacher Training Academy at Cerritos. The Teacher Training Academy at Cerritos graduated more than five hundred students after five years of existence. Similar efforts have proved fruitful across the state and the country. Though not all in education, science, technology, engineering, and mathematics (STEM) programs have focused on the recruitment of students of color from community colleges.

In addition to these efforts, California community colleges and the University of California established nine areas of collaboration in a memorandum of understanding that seeks to increase the transferability of students (Zamani, 2001). Other innovative cooperative programs entail articulation transfer agreements between community colleges and out-of-state private colleges (Wolf-Wendel, Twombly, Morphew, and Sopcich, 2004). These rare out-of-state articulation agreements have proven successful by breaching the common in-state transferability pipeline.

NEW DIRECTIONS FOR STUDENT SERVICES • DOI: 10.1002/ss

Transferring to a Research-Extensive University: The Academic Year Research Experience (AYRE) Program

A review of research reveals that most transitory programs established by four-year institutions for entering community college students are discipline-based programs. Unlike teacher training or STEM programs, the Academic Year Research Experience (AYRE) program seeks specifically to increase the number of students of color, regardless of discipline, at the University of Illinois at Urbana-Champaign.

The Program's Purpose. The Academic Year Research Experience Program (AYRE) is funded and managed by the Educational Equity Programs Office at the University of Illinois, Urbana-Champaign (UIUC). The program was developed to facilitate the transition of freshmen and sophomores in becoming active participants in research at UIUC. AYRE provides the opportunity for students to cultivate skills and become acquainted with the academic culture of UIUC so as to help them successfully complete the bachelor's degree and pursue postbaccalaureate study.

Eligibility. The course is open to freshman and sophomore students from UIUC and, recently, Parkland College, the neighboring feeder community college. Students are expected to have completed at least fifteen and no more than sixty-five credit hours and have a minimum 2.5 GPA. The AYRE staff works with UIUC representatives and Parkland College counselors to identify prospective transfer students as probable candidates for the program. Once identified, candidates must submit an application, a letter of recommendation, statement of purpose, and unofficial college transcripts. Eligible students attend a weekly two-hour seminar during UIUC's spring semester.

Weekly Seminar. Taught by a doctoral student in education, the course is worth up to four UIUC credit hours and consists of academic work and research that will assist students in becoming familiar with the academic culture of UIUC and similar research-extensive universities. Class sessions entail writing workshops, visits by university administrators, trips to the library, and critical-thinking activities intended to improve skills necessary for academic success at UIUC. This format enables the instructor to decrease the myths regarding class registration, financial aid, counseling, and student services offered on campus. For Parkland College students, the course is deliberate in attempting to lessen the transfer and cultural shock commonly experienced by students of color and former community college students (Wolf-Wendel, Twombly, Morphew, and Sopcich, 2004). Parkland students earn college credit at UIUC, yet are not required to transfer to UIUC.

Benefits of the Program. Participants who complete AYRE successfully are provided the opportunity to participate in the UIUC Summer Research Opportunities Program (SROP). SROP provides academically competitive students with nine weeks of summer research under the direction of a research

NEW DIRECTIONS FOR STUDENT SERVICES • DOI: 10.1002/ss

faculty member at UIUC. SROP students are primed to conduct research and to pursue graduate study. Each participant receives a stipend, a housing allowance, a meal allowance, GRE preparation (upperclassmen only), classes in research-writing skills, books and materials, and participation in an academic conference at a Committee on Institutional Cooperation (CIC) institution in an award package valued at approximately $7,000. Participants are able to develop important relationships with key faculty and administrators in their colleges, intended program of study, and on campus that are necessary as they prepare for advanced study. SROP participants are also able to establish important relationships with other students in their majors who attend colleges and universities from across the United States and Puerto Rico. Finally, students who have completed AYRE and SROP are highly sought after by graduate and professional programs throughout the country.

AYRE students are introduced to the numerous resources available to students at UIUC as well as being able to improve their writing, research, presentation, and other academic skills. As participants, AYRE students have an opportunity to gain more immediate access to information needed to become successful as an undergraduate and in pursuing postbaccalaureate study.

Benefits of AYRE for Community College Transfer Students. In a recent study conducted by Perez and Aragon (2005), students of color from Parkland Community College were interviewed for the purpose of obtaining their perceptions of AYRE. The Parkland students included five women and one male. All were students of color. Students spoke favorably about their experiences with the program, highlighting some of the following observations about their participation:

- Student perceptions of the UIUC racial climate was enhanced
- Students spoke favorably of the UIUC administration
- Students became familiar with university facilities, such as the library, admissions, and financial aid offices
- AYRE successfully introduced students of color to the social culture of a research-extensive university
- The academic expectations of UIUC were demystified
- Students anticipate transferring to UIUC

It appears that the AYRE program is having a positive influence on students' understanding about the four-year UIUC program by introducing students of color from the local community college to the culture and expectations of UIUC. In addition, student perceptions of what is referred to as campus racial climate were enhanced (Gurin and others, 2002; Hurtado, Milem, Clayton-Pederson, and Allen, 1998). Longitudinal data collected by the Educational Equity Programs Office show that the AYRE participants who initially start their academic program at UIUC are successfully completing their bachelor's degree and continuing on for postbaccalaureate study. Because this program has only recently invited students of color from community colleges who desire to transfer to UIUC, it is too early to determine if it will have the same long-term effects for them.

First-semester student success courses should not be limited to freshman enrolled at four-year institutions or community colleges. Our results suggest that similar programs should be established for community college students. Most poignant, unlike most student success courses and programs (Hagedorn and Cepeda, 2004), AYRE deliberately enrolls community college students before they officially enroll in a four-year, research-extensive university. As a result of including community college students earlier, the Educational Equity Programs Office specifically seeks to increase the persistence of students of color before they enter research-extensive universities by integrating them earlier in the enrollment process.

References

Ahumada, M. M. "Inter-Institutional Transfer and Articulation: The Role of Data Bases and Information Systems." *Community College Journal of Research and Practice,* 1993, 17(2), 141–152.

American Association of Colleges for Teacher Education (AACTE). *The Community College Role in Teacher Education: A Case for Collaboration.* Washington, D.C.: American Association of Colleges for Teacher Education, 2002.

American Association of Community Colleges (AACC). *Improving Access to the Baccalaureate.* Washington, D.C.: Community College Press, 2004.

American Council on Education (ACE). *Access and Persistence: Findings from 10 years of Longitudinal Research on Students.* Washington, D.C.: American Council on Education, 2002.

Bettinger, E. P., and Long, B. T. "Remediation at the Community College: Student Participation and Outcomes." In C. Kozeracki (ed.), *Responding to the Challenges of Developmental Education.* New Directions for Community Colleges, no. 129. San Francisco: Jossey-Bass, 2005.

Brint, S. "Few Remaining Dreams: Community Colleges Since 1985." *Annals of the American Academy of Political Science and Social Science,* Mar. 2003, 386, 16–37.

Bryant, A. N. "Community College Students: Recent Findings and Trends." *Community College Review,* 2001, 29(3), 77–93.

Callan, P. M. "Stewards of Opportunity: America's Public Community Colleges." *Daedalus,* 1997, 126(4), 95–112.

Carlan, P. E., and Byxbe, F. R. "Community Colleges Under the Microscope: An Analysis of Performance Predictors for Native and Transfer Students." *Community College Review,* 2000, 28(2), 27–42.

Cejda, B. D. "An Examination of Transfer Shock in Academic Disciplines." *Community College Journal of Research and Practice,* 1997, 21(3), 379–389.

Cofer, J., and Somers, P. "What Influences Student Persistence at Two-Year Colleges?" *Community College Review,* 2001, 29(3), 56–76.

Cohen, A. M., and Brawer, F. B. *The American Community College.* (4th ed.) San Francisco: Jossey-Bass, 2003.

Dowd, A. C. "From Access to Outcome Reality: Revitalizing the Democratic Mission of Community Colleges." *Annals of the American Academy of Political Science and Social Science,* Mar. 2003, 386, 92–119.

Glass, J. C., Jr., and Harrington, A. R. "Academic Performance of Community College Transfer Students and 'Native' Students at a Large State University." *Community College Journal of Research and Practice,* 2002, 26(5), 415–431.

Gurin, P., and others. "Diversity and Higher Education: Theory and Impact on Education Outcomes." *Harvard Educational Review,* 2002, *72*(3), 330–366.

Hagedorn, L. S., and Cepeda, R. "Serving Los Angeles: Urban Community Colleges and Educational Success Among Latino Students." *Community College Journal of Research and Practice,* 2004, *28*(3), 199–211.

Hagedorn, L. S., Newman, F., and Duffy, J. "Taking the Golden State Path to Teacher Education: California Partnerships Among Two-Year Colleges and University Centers." In B. K. Townsend and J. M. Ignash (eds.), *The Role of the Community College in Teacher Education.* New Directions for Community Colleges, no. 121. San Francisco: Jossey-Bass, 2003.

Hurtado, S., Milem, J. F., Clayton-Pedersen, A. R., and Allen, W. "Enhancing Campus Climates for Racial/Ethnic Diversity: Educational Policy and Practice." *Review of Higher Education,* 1998, *21*(3), 279–302.

Hutcheson, P. A. "Reconsidering the Community College." *History of Education Quarterly,* 1999, *39*(3), 307–320.

Laanan, F. S. "Making the Transition: Understanding the Adjustment Process of Community College Transfer Students." *Community College Review,* 1996, *23*(4) 69–85.

Laanan, F. S. "Transfer Student Adjustment." In F. S. Laanan (ed.), *Transfer Students: Trends and Issues.* New Directions for Community Colleges, no. 114. San Francisco: Jossey-Bass, 2001.

Laanan, F. S. "Degree Aspirations of Two-Year College Students." *Community College Journal of Research and Practice,* 2003, *27,* 495–518.

Laanan, F. S. "Studying Transfer Students: Part I: Instrument Design and Implications." *Community College Journal of Research and Practice,* 2004, *28*(4), 331–351.

National Center for Education Statistics (NCES). *Postsecondary Education, Tables 206 and 207.* Washington, D.C.: National Center for Education Statistics. 2004. http://nces.ed.gov/programs/digest/d04/lt3.asp#c3a_1. Accessed Oct. 30, 2005.

Ornelas, A., and Solórzano, D. "Transfer Conditions of Latina/o Community College Students: A Single Institution Case Study." *Community College Journal of Research and Practice.* 2004, *28*(3), 233–248.

Pascarella, E., and Terenzini, P. *How College Affects Students: Findings and Insights from Twenty Years of Research.* San Francisco: Jossey-Bass, 1991.

Perez, M. R., and Aragon, S. A. *Making It to the Big Ten: Minority Student Perceptions of One University Transfer Initiative.* Unpublished manuscript, 2005.

Rendón, L. I., Jalomo, R., Jr., and Nora, A. "Theoretical Considerations in the Study of Minority Student Retention in Higher Education." In J. M. Braxton (ed.), *Reworking the Student Departure Puzzle.* Nashville: Vanderbilt University Press, 2000.

St. John, E. P., and Starkey, J. "The Influence of Costs on Persistence by Traditional College-Aged Students in Community College." *Community College Journal of Research and Practice,* 1994, *18*(2), 201–213.

Solórzano, D., Rivas, M. A., and Velez, V. N. "Community College as a Pathway to Chicana/o Doctorate Production." *Latino Policy and Issues Brief 11.* Los Angles: UCLA Chicano Studies Research Center, 2005.

Stovall, M. "Using Success Courses for Promoting Persistence and Completion." In S. R. Aragon (ed.), *Beyond Access: Methods and Models for Increasing Retention and Learning Success Among Minority Students.* New Directions for Community Colleges, no. 112. San Francisco: Jossey-Bass, 2000.

Swail, W. S., Redd, K. E., and Perna L. W. *Retaining Minority Students in Higher Education: A Framework for Success.* ASHE-ERIC Higher Education Report, 2003.

Townsend, B. K., Bragg, D., and Kinnick, M. "Who Writes the Most About Community Colleges? An Analysis of Selected Academic and Practitioner-Oriented Journals." *Community College Journal of Research and Practice,* 2003, *27*(1), 41–49.

Townsend, B. K., and Ignash, J. M. "Evaluating State-Level Articulation Agreements According to Good Practice." *Community College Review,* 2000, *28*(3), 1–21.

Welsh, J. F. "Assessing the Transfer Function: Benchmarking Best Practices from the State of Higher Education Agencies." *Assessment and Evaluation in Higher Education,* 2002, 27(3), 257–268.

Welsh. J. F., and Kjorlien, C. "State Support for Interinstitutional Transfer and Articulation: The Impact of Databases and Information Systems." *Community College Journal of Research and Practice,* 2001, 25(4), 313–332.

Wolf-Wendel, L., Twombly, S., Morphew, C., and Sopcich, J. "From the Barrio to the Bucolic: The Student Transfer Experience from HSIs to Smith College." *Community College Journal of Research and Practice,* 2004, 29, 213–231.

Wright, L. M., and Middleberg, R. "Lessons from a Long-Term Collaboration." In D. McGrath (ed.), *Creating and Benefiting from Institutional Collaboration: Models for Success.* New Directions for Community Colleges, no. 103. San Francisco, Jossey-Bass, 1998.

Zamani, E. M. "Institutional Responses to Barriers to the Transfer Process." In F. S. Laanan (ed.), *Transfer Students: Trends and Issues.* New Directions for Community Colleges, no. 114. San Francisco: Jossey-Bass, 2001, 15–24.

STEVEN R. ARAGON *is associate professor in the Department of Human Resource Education at the University of Illinois at Urbana-Champaign. Dr. Aragon specializes in postsecondary education (community college), teaching and learning models for postsecondary minority and nontraditional students, and minority student development in community college settings.*

MARIO RIOS PEREZ *is a doctoral candidate in Educational Policy Studies at the University of Illinois at Urbana-Champaign. He specializes in the history of American education and in issues of access and equity in higher education policy.*

NEW DIRECTIONS FOR STUDENT SERVICES • DOI: 10.1002/ss

8

This chapter presents a hypothetical situation related to students who are displaced by Hurricane Katrina. It focuses on transition issues for the students as they are relocated to a new college for an undetermined length of time.

Forced Transitions: The Impact of Natural Disasters and Other Events on College Students

John H. Schuh, Frankie Santos Laanan

At the time this volume was being prepared, Hurricane Katrina and Hurricane Rita hit the Gulf States, causing everything from inconvenience at some colleges and universities to such destruction and havoc that the future of several institutions is very much in doubt. That is, it is unclear if or when they may reopen. This chapter is designed to focus on how events such as natural disasters create transition problems and issues for students that must be resolved for them to continue their education on a relatively uninterrupted basis. We have chosen to identify salient issues related to students and provide some advice on how students might best be served when their academic careers undergo such dramatic disruption. This chapter is not designed to provide a checklist for student affairs administrators who deal with such problems; instead, we have chosen to look at some conceptual and general issues related to forced transitions. In addition, the chapter has not been crafted to deal with institutional issues, such as developing and implementing a plan for renovation of damaged faculties, covering financial obligations, or how researchers can sustain their scholarly inquiry when their laboratories or data are ruined. As time passes, we anticipate that researchers and others who study college students will develop empirical studies that will provide details about students who experience forced transitions.

NEW DIRECTIONS FOR STUDENT SERVICES, no. 114, Summer 2006 © Wiley Periodicals, Inc.
Published online in Wiley InterScience (www.interscience.wiley.com) • DOI: 10.1002/ss.210

93

A Scenario Involving a Hypothetical Student

Sean, who had been planning to enroll as a first-year student at an institution of higher education in New Orleans, checked final plans to travel to the institution and begin coursework. Sean is an out-of-state student. With personal belongings shipped ahead, all Sean needed to do was to hop on a plane, travel to New Orleans, and get established in the new environment. A few days after arriving, and barely after moving into a residence hall on campus, Sean is relocated to Rolling Hills College (a pseudonym), an institution three hundred miles from New Orleans, in anticipation of Hurricane Katrina. Relocated to a new college, with just a few belongings, Sean learned that the institution in New Orleans has suffered severe damage and no one is quite sure when the college will reopen. Now located in a strange place not of his choosing, our first-year student is faced with making the best of a new situation shortly after starting the transition process at the college of his choice in New Orleans. Rolling Hills College (RHC) is similar to Sean's college in terms of curriculum, and since both institutions are private, the transition presumably would not have been as complex had the students been taken to a public university. Sean is determined to continue the semester at the new college regardless of the bewildering set of experiences of the past few days. Going home at this point is not an option, although Sean has thought about doing just that.

Sean's Dilemmas

The series of problems encountered by Sean create an incredibly difficult situation for this student and the others displaced from New Orleans. Kuh (2004) described the experience of first-year students this way: "For many students, especially first-generation students and those living away from home for the first time, the initial weeks of the first academic term are like living in a foreign land" (p. 86). Barely settled in a new environment, Sean has had to pick up and go to college somewhere else, at least for the foreseeable future. For Sean this means living in a second foreign land in a matter of weeks.

While complex transitions and displacements are not common in higher education in the United States, they do occur with a certain degree of regularity, as measured by hurricane activity in the gulf states, tornadoes in the Midwest, earthquakes in California, and blizzards, flooding, and other forms of natural disasters that are unpredictable as to when they might strike and the severity of the havoc they will wreak. Nevertheless, there are some issues that student affairs practitioners should think through as they prepare to respond to student needs in situations where the routine activities of the campus are significantly disrupted for an extended period of time. In this chapter we look at foundational issues for institutions that receive displaced students. We will comment on Sean's situation and identify some of the issues that need to be addressed.

New Directions for Student Services • DOI: 10.1002/ss

Using Theory to Inform Practice

Theory can be helpful in understanding the challenges that Sean and the displaced New Orleans students will be going through as they evacuate to a new college. One of the options that Sean and the other students might consider is to drop out of college temporarily. That is, they might come to the conclusion that they ought to wait until the situation is settled. By that we mean that their college has been repaired and reopens. The risk, of course, is that if they drop out now, they may not return.

The work of Schlossberg (1984) is especially helpful in framing what Sean and the displaced New Orleans students will be experiencing. First, the transition they will be making from their college in New Orleans to their new college can be classified as an unanticipated transition; that is, what they have experienced is a series of events that "are not predictable or scheduled" (Evans, Forney and Guido-DeBrito, 1998, p. 112). At the risk of oversimplifying the situation, support for the students is essential as they develop strategies to managing the transitions they face. RHC's approach to helping them deal with the forced transition will be absolutely crucial.

Schlossberg's work on the concept of mattering also is instructive. Mattering in this case is an important concept "because when students feel that someone in the institution cares about them, takes an interest in them, and pays attention to their experience, they feel they matter" (Braxton, 2003, p. 324). By leaving their college in New Orleans, the students are leaving what has become familiar and they are moving to a college not of their choosing. They will need to feel that someone at the new college cares about them and is welcoming them to their new surroundings.

Tinto's theory of academic departure can also be useful in understanding Sean's situation upon arrival. Students need to feel as though they are connected to their college in an academic and social sense to persist. According to this theory, "The more academically and socially involved individuals are—that is, the more they interact with other students and faculty—the more likely they are to persist" (Tinto, 1998, p. 168). For Sean this means that interacting with students and faculty at the new college will be essential. Sean and the other displaced students from New Orleans are going to have to get involved in the new college as quickly as they can, but in the backs of their minds will be that their stay is going to be temporary because they plan to return to New Orleans when the college there is repaired. However, they might have to stay for a year, so they will need to make connections. This could be particularly difficult if the new college makes extensive use of learning communities. Making connections at the new college could be difficult if students have short-term plans to withdraw from the temporary college experience in hopes to return to their original college or university in New Orleans. These issues will have an effect on many levels of adjustment and transition such as social, academic, and personal.

NEW DIRECTIONS FOR STUDENT SERVICES • DOI: 10.1002/ss

Communications with Family Members

One of the very first issues that needs to be addressed is to make certain that students have arrived safely and securely at the receiving institution and that family members are informed about the situation. In the case of Sean, all the first-year students from Sean's college were bused to RHC. RHC is similar to Sean's college in terms of curriculum, and since both institutions are private, the transition presumably would not have been as complex had the students been taken to a public university.

Initial communications. The first thing that needs to be addressed is to make sure that the family members of the students who have been relocated are notified as to where their students have been taken and how they can contact their students. A bank of phones could be set up to handle this requirement. Often the alumni association or fundraising office have such a bank of phones, and the relocated students should be taken there to contact their family members. Even if they claim to have cell phones or have contacted their parents, the calls should be made with institutional representatives available to answer any questions that the family members may have.

Telephone number. Sean has a cell phone, but he will need a telephone number while enrolled at RHC so that people on campus can remain in contact with him. The room that Sean will be living in has a telephone number as well as an online connection to the Internet. The telephone number needs to be provided to students as they make their first call to their families so that family members can call their students in the residence hall as they need to, rather than relying on cell phone service.

Mailing address. In addition to having made the first contact from RHC, Sean and the other students will have to have mailing addresses—for both U.S. postal service and electronic mail. Institutional representatives can provide these. Happily enough, all students have mailboxes in the student union, and box numbers are assigned to the displaced students so they can receive mail through the U.S. postal service as well as through campus mail. Electronic mailing addresses also should be established for the displaced students at RHC. This is so they can receive routine communications while they are on campus, such as broadcast electronic messages that are sent to all RHC students.

Housing

Concomitant with notifying family members about the students' whereabouts is to provide places for them to live. If space is available in a campus residence hall situation, the students can move in upon arrival on campus. If residence hall space is not available, then other options need to be arranged in advance of the students' arrival in order to provide as smooth a transition as possible. Other options include the institution's hotel if it has one, an empty fraternity or sorority house (assuming that the facility is in good condition and ready for occupancy), hotel or motel space in the local community, or even the homes or apartments of faculty and staff members. If none of these options are available, then the next best option, although not desirable, is to convert common area space in the campus residence halls to student quarters. At times, overflow housing is used on campuses that have greater demand for space than is available but this is not desirable. Converting space means that beds, desks, and storage for clothing and other items need to be provided, as well as communications connections, including telephones and Internet. Doing this on almost no notice is very demanding and may not be feasible. Our recommendation is that if suitable housing is not available for displaced students, then careful consideration should be given to placing the students at another institution. Adding a third person to a double-occupancy room is another option, although this choice has a variety of problems associated with it, including potentially violating health and fire codes as well as creating an uncomfortable living situation for all three students.

Contracts. Once students have been placed in housing, and in Sean's case enough housing was available for all of the students to live on campus, then the next issue that has to be considered is financial. Housing does not come without cost. Extra students potentially mean extra staff if buildings out of service have to be opened, as well as more work for housekeeping and maintenance staff. The additional communications lines bring additional cost, as will food service for the displaced students. The major question is, who will pay the additional costs, and in what form? Will Sean and the other displaced students be billed for the costs? If so, will it be on a daily basis? Or, will Sean's college be billed? What if the displaced students want to leave campus housing and move into other accommodations off campus? Are they bound to stay in the residence halls on campus at RHC? While some of these questions might seem to be heartless, they need to be resolved; if they are not, RHC will have to cover the costs, and what that means, realistically, is that the room-and-board payments of the permanent students attending RHC will be subsidizing Sean and the other displaced students.

Food service. RHC has adequate capacity to provide food service for Sean and the other students from New Orleans. But as is the case with housing, who will pay the cost of food service? What food-service plan is available to the displaced students? Students at RHC have a choice of three meal plans. Will that also be the case for the displaced students? The simplest decision is to offer the same choices to the displaced students and charge them a daily rate for food service. Of course, one returns to the question of who will pay the bill—the students themselves or their college in New Orleans?

Roommates. Assuming spaces are available on campus, the issue then becomes one of whether the displaced students would be housed together as much as possible or should they be dispersed throughout the residence halls. Available space will dictate the answer to this question to a certain extent, but if space is available, which is the better approach? Our view is that the students ought to be housed as much together as possible so it is easy to contact them and hold meetings as necessary. They can develop support for each other and as they get to know students from RHC, they will begin to widen their network of acquaintances.

Academic Advising

Sean and the other displaced students will need academic advising to be directed to courses that are appropriate for them. For first-year students, that may be less complex than for upper-class students; on the other hand, it is not advisable for them to enroll in just any course that has vacant seats.

Enrollment in Which Courses? Sean plans to major in chemistry, which includes a basic curriculum of courses followed by electives. In advising this first-year student, the advisor has to find courses in Sean's major that are equivalent to the courses he would have taken at the college in New Orleans. In addition, general education courses should be identified for Sean. The problem, of course, is that seats in these courses have to be available or new sections have to be created. One can argue that filling vacant seats costs next to nothing for RHC, but creating new sections can be expensive, unless it is possible to find faculty members from Sean's college in New Orleans to teach them. Of course, bringing faculty from New Orleans to RHC has some problems associated with it, including finding living quarters for these people and their family members, providing office space and other support for them, and trying to integrate them into the RHC faculty for as long as they are in the community. Just to add to the problems of curriculum, suppose Sean's college has a mandatory orientation course for first-year students. Is it offered at RHC? If so, how meaningful could it be since the students are located three hundred miles from campus? As a graduation requirement, could it be waived because of the special circumstance? These questions would have to be answered, probably once the college in New Orleans reopens.

Prerequisites. RHC has prerequisites for many courses and makes placements in other courses based on tests administered to students before enrollment. This is especially true for courses in mathematics and foreign languages. What if the students who have been moved to RHC do not have the appropriate prerequisites? Obtaining waivers may not be a problem, but the issue has more to do with students being at an appropriate level of knowledge to benefit from the course. If they are not, they may not benefit from the course, or they may harm their grade-point average with a subpar grade. Handling appropriate course placements is an issue that has to be resolved.

Missed Term Work? If, as was the case at RHC, the term began two weeks before Sean and the other displaced students arrived, some kind of accommodation will have to be made for them to account for the coursework they have missed. Make-up sessions and tutoring might be the only way to provide assistance for them, but this comes at a cost. Who will pay for the extra services? In the abstract, if the disaster had occurred much beyond the first couple of weeks of school, it would be very difficult to try

NEW DIRECTIONS FOR STUDENT SERVICES • DOI: 10.1002/ss

to integrate the students from New Orleans into existing class sections. Creating new sections may or may not be particularly difficult, depending on the extent to which appropriate instructors and space could be identified, but this would come with substantial cost. In the discussion of costs below, this matter will be developed.

Transfer Policies. Finally, for the purposes of enrollment and grading, are the displaced students considered to be RHC students, or students of the college in New Orleans? If they are considered to be RHC students, then the grades and course credit will ultimately have to be transferred to the college in New Orleans. That may cause additional problems, so thought will have to be given as to how transfer credit will be awarded. What if displaced students take courses in disciplines that are not offered at the college in New Orleans? Will they still receive full credit? Certainly, the students will need to be afforded some accommodations, but the institution's policies might be violated if, for example, students take courses in disciplines not offered at the original institution. This issue also will need to be resolved.

Financial Issues

As we have suggested, the challenges of determining who will pay for what for the students in forced transition are complex. One option is for the students to pay their college in New Orleans as if they were still enrolled and living on campus, and for the college in New Orleans to reimburse RHC for the entire expenses attendant with the displaced students. That works as long as the costs are equivalent. What if it costs more to enroll and house the students at RHC than would have been the case at the New Orleans college? Who pays the difference? What if it costs less? Does someone get a refund? If so, does it go to the students individually or the college in New Orleans?

Transitional Support. Sean lost almost everything in the hurricane. All of his personal items in the residence hall in New Orleans were lost. Such was the case for everyone. So, they left with the clothes on their backs, their cell phones if they had them, and in most cases, but not all, their wallets. As they arrived at RHC they had nothing. Support for them to purchase new items—clothes, personal hygiene items, computer equipment, and so on—has to be arranged in a hurry. In some cases the students may have had insurance or their parents' insurance policies may have covered their losses, but in other cases that form of assistance is likely not available. Even if it was, it might be days before help in the form of cash or a check to buy new things would arrive. Short of leaving this problem to each student, what can be done?

Cost differentials. In our hypothetical situation, we assumed that students had left a private institution and were received by a private institution. But what if they had left a private institution and went to a public institution? What if they are out-of-state students at the new, public institution? What tuition would they pay? What if the costs were tremendously different, such as the difference between attending an in-state public institution and having to go to a private institution where tuition is substantially greater? To make our example simple, we have tried to develop a scenario where the costs would be equivalent, but in actuality the potential for them to be substantially different is quite realistic. If that is the case, how will the difference in costs be managed?

Financial aid. Sean's financial aid package included quite a bit of institutional aid that was designed to lower the cost of attendance. Since Sean comes from modest financial circumstances, family support is not available to help manage the costs of attending a more expensive institution. Would RHC be willing to provide institutional support to help with the cost of attendance? Might federal loans be available? Sean had not applied for them but now might be forced to seek outside help. These challenges add to the stress of being displaced from New Orleans to RHC.

Orientation

Obviously, Sean and the other displaced students need to have an orientation to RHC. This will need to be accomplished just as soon as possible after their arrival on campus. The problem for them, of course, is to keep everything straight, because they would have just participated in an orientation process to their college in New Orleans. Most important, the content of the orientation at RHC would have to be tailored to their needs as students who will be at RHC for a limited period of time, although that could be an entire year, depending on how quickly their college in New Orleans can be repaired. The New Orleans students need to learn how things are done at RHC and be able not to get that confused with what they have just learned about how things are done at their college in New Orleans.

A difficult dimension of orientation is that RHC students have just begun to establish friendships and form their social groups. Sean and the other displaced students are faced with the challenge of having to connect with RHC students after that process has begun. Some special events for the students from New Orleans will need to be held, and students from RHC will have to be encouraged to attend so that the New Orleans students can begin to connect with them.

A special role will have to be developed for orientation assistants (OAs) from RHC who might be able to help in the connecting process. RHC has an orientation course, but it is probably not appropriate for the New Orleans students to take it, since it goes into substantial depth about RHC and, besides, it began two weeks ago. The OAs can help with the orientation program for the New Orleans students and can even plan special events to help them get connected with RHC so their stay is more comfortable. Unfortunately, the OAs appointments were for just the week prior to and during the week classes began, so they will need to be paid an extra stipend for their additional assignment. How this is to be paid for will have to be determined.

NEW DIRECTIONS FOR STUDENT SERVICES • DOI: 10.1002/ss

Student Work

Some of the students from New Orleans had campus-based jobs that were designed not only to provide them with some extra money but also to help them get connected with faculty and staff members. In Sean's case, an internship was set up on campus in the lab of a chemistry instructor. Since Sean has been thinking about majoring in chemistry, this assistantship was designed to provide an inside look at the academic discipline. Obviously, with the move to RHC, that assistantship is no longer available. Or is it? Can RHC develop additional student assistantships for those who are interested, even though they may be at RHC for just a semester or two? If the existing RHC assistantships are paid for by grants, can the grants absorb additional personnel costs? If they are paid for by RHC, can the college handle the extra costs? These issues will have to be determined as soon as possible. Assistantships for undergraduate students can be extremely growth producing for students (see Kuh, Kinzie, Schuh, and Whitt, 2005), and some action needs to be taken so that the New Orleans students do not miss this valuable experience.

Other students from New Orleans had jobs on or off campus to help defray their expenses related to going to college. Can RHC create jobs for these students or help them find employment off campus, even though they may only be available to work for a semester? The answers to these questions are unknown, but the questions speak to the complexity of having hundreds of new students arrive on such short notice.

Counseling Support

Counseling support is also necessary for the students who have been moved to RHC. They have undergone a traumatic experience and, depending on where their homes were, their families may have suffered dramatic losses, not only of their homes and possessions, but also potentially of their health and even the lives of their loved ones. How long the New Orleans students might need special counseling help is not clear, but plans will need to be developed so that they can receive counseling while they are enrolled at RHC beyond what normally might be available there. This might take the form of support groups or other group interventions that could be made available to them.

Permanent Transfer

Finally, some students may like RHC so well that they may choose to transfer permanently. In that circumstance, are there any special conditions? The purpose of providing a place for Sean and the New Orleans students to enroll was not a thinly veiled attempt at "poaching" students by RHC. But what if the students want to stay rather than to return to New Orleans? Can they? Would they have to transfer through a more formal process than the one that led them to RHC under the press of the hurricane? These questions also need to be addressed as the time approaches for the students to return to New Orleans.

A Final Note

The goal of this chapter was to present a hypothetical scenario of what some college students are currently facing as a result of the recent natural disaster of Hurricane Katrina. We are reminded that educational organizations must be flexible and prepared for unexpected events and disruptions caused by nature. The rebuilding of institutions, facilities, programs, and services is important for the sustainability of a college's or university's legacy and unique place among America's higher education institutions. More important, it is the fragile lives of students that must be a priority in terms of reducing the stress of an unexpected adjustment and forced transitions. Only time will tell of the lessons learned that will help inform student services professionals to be better prepared to serve students during these challenging situations. Maintaining flexible and creative approaches to addressing the emerging issues and needs will be key to a productive and rewarding future for institutions and their staff, their students, and their communities.

References

Braxton, J. M. "Student Success." In S. R. Komives, D. B. Woodard, Jr., and Associates (eds.), *Student Services: A Handbook for the Profession.* (4th ed.) San Francisco: Jossey-Bass, 2003.

Evans, N. J., Forney, D. S., and Guido-DiBrito, F. *Student Development in College: Theory, Research, and Practice.* San Francisco: Jossey-Bass, 1998.

Kuh, G. D. "Student Engagement in the First Year of College." In M. L. Upcraft, J. N. Gardner, B. O. Barefoot, and Associates, *Challenging and Supporting the First-Year Student: A Handbook for Improving the First Year of College.* San Francisco: Jossey-Bass, 2004.

Kuh, G. D., Kinzie, J., Schuh, J. H., and Whitt, E. J. *Student Success in College: Creating Conditions That Matter.* San Francisco: Jossey-Bass, 2005.

Schlossberg, N. *Counseling Adults in Transition.* New York: Springer, 1984.

Tinto, V. "Colleges as Communities." *Review of Higher Education,* 1998, *21,* 167–177.

JOHN H. SCHUH is a distinguished professor and Frankie Santos Laanan is associate professor, both in the Department of Educational Leadership and Policy Studies at Iowa State University.

INDEX

103

Back Issue/Subscription Order Form

Copy or detach and send to:

Jossey-Bass, A Wiley Imprint, 989 Market Street, San Francisco CA, 94103-1741

Call or fax toll-free: Phone 888-378-2537 6:30AM – 3PM PST; Fax 888-481-2665

Back Issues: Please send me the following issues at $27 each

(Important: please include ISBN number for each issue.)

_____

_____

_____

$ _____   Total for single issues

$ _____   SHIPPING CHARGES: SURFACE   Domestic Canadian

| | | First Item | $5.00 | $6.00 |
| | | Each Add'l Item | $3.00 | $1.50 |

For next-day and second-day delivery rates, call the number listed above.

Subscriptions   Please __ start __ renew my subscription to *New Directions for Student Services* for the year 2____ at the following rate:

U.S.	__ Individual $75	__ Institutional $180
Canada	__ Individual $75	__ Institutional $220
All Others	__ Individual $99	__ Institutional $254

For more information about online subscriptions visit
www.wileyinterscience.com

$ Total single issues and subscriptions (Add appropriate sales tax for your state for single issue orders. No sales tax for U.S. subscriptions. Canadian residents, add GST for subscriptions and single issues.)

__Payment enclosed (U.S. check or money order only)

__VISA __ MC __ AmEx Card #_____Exp.Date_____

Signature _____ Day Phone _____

__Bill Me (U.S. institutional orders only. Purchase order required.)

Purchase order # _____

Federal Tax ID13559302   **GST 89102 8052**

Name _____

Address _____

_____

Phone _____ E-mail _____

For more information about Jossey-Bass, visit our Web site at **www.josseybass.com**

OTHER TITLES AVAILABLE IN THE
New Directions for Student Services Series
JOHN H. SCHUH, EDITOR-IN-CHIEF
ELIZABETH J. WHITT, ASSOCIATE EDITOR

SS113   Gambling on Campus
        George S. McClellan, Thomas W. Hardy, Jim Caswell
        Gambling has become a serious concern on college campuses, fueled by the
        surge of online gaming and the national poker craze, and is no longer a
        fringe activity. This informative issue includes perspectives from students,
        suggestions for research, frameworks for campus policy development, and
        case studies of education and intervention. Anyone interested in supporting
        student success must be informed about gambling on campus.
        ISBN: 0-7879-8597-X

SS112   Technology in Student Affairs: Supporting Student Learning and Services
        Kevin Kruger
        Information technology has helped create a 24/7 self-service way for
        students to interact with campus administrative functions, whether they're
        on campus or distance learners. And new technologies could move beyond
        administrative into student learning and development. This volume is not a
        review of current technology in student affairs. Rather, it focuses on how
        technology is changing the organization of student affairs, how to use it
        effectively, and how lines are blurring between campus-based and distance
        learning.
        ISBN: 0-7879-8362-4

SS111   Gender Identity and Sexual Orientation: Research, Policy, and Personal
        Perspectives
        Ronni L. Sanlo
        Lesbian, gay, bisexual, and transgender people have experienced
        homophobia, discrimination, exclusion, and marginalization in the academy,
        from subtle to overt. Yet LGBT people have been a vital part of the history of
        American higher education. This volume describes current issues, research,
        and policies, and it offers ways for institutions to support and foster the
        success of LGBT students, faculty, and staff.
        ISBN: 0-7879-8328-4

SS110   Developing Social Justice Allies
        Robert D. Reason, Ellen M. Broido, Tracy L. Davis, Nancy J. Evans
        Social justice allies are individuals from dominant groups (for example,
        whites, heterosexuals, men) who work to end the oppression of target group
        members (people of color, homosexuals, women). Student affairs
        professionals have a history of philosophical commitment to social justice,
        and this volume strives to provide the theoretical foundation and practical
        strategies to encourage the development of social justice and civil rights
        allies among students and colleagues.
        ISBN: 0-7879-8077-3

SS109   Serving Native American Students
        Mary Jo Tippeconnic Fox, Shelly C. Lowe, George S. McClellan
        The increasing Native American enrollment on campuses nationwide is
        something to celebrate; however, the retention rate for Native American
        students is the lowest in higher education, a point of tremendous concern.
        This volume's authors—most of them Native American—address topics such
        as enrollment trends, campus experiences, cultural traditions, student
        services, ignorance about Indian country issues, expectations of tribal
        leaders and parents, and other challenges and opportunities encountered by
        Native students.
        ISBN: 0-7879-7971-6

**NEW DIRECTIONS FOR STUDENT SERVICES
IS NOW AVAILABLE ONLINE AT WILEY INTERSCIENCE**

What is Wiley InterScience?

Wiley InterScience is the dynamic online content service from John Wiley & Sons delivering the full text of over 300 leading scientific, technical, medical, and professional journals, plus major reference works, the acclaimed *Current Protocols* laboratory manuals, and even the full text of select Wiley print books online.

What are some special features of Wiley InterScience?

Wiley InterScience Alerts is a service that delivers table of contents via e-mail for any journal available on Wiley InterScience as soon as a new issue is published online.

Early View is Wiley's exclusive service presenting individual articles online as soon as they are ready, even before the release of the compiled print issue. These articles are complete, peer-reviewed, and citable.

CrossRef is the innovative multi-publisher reference linking system enabling readers to move seamlessly from a reference in a journal article to the cited publication, typically located on a different server and published by a different publisher.

How can I access Wiley InterScience?

Visit http://www.interscience.wiley.com

Guest Users can browse Wiley InterScience for unrestricted access to journal Tables of Contents and Article Abstracts, or use the powerful search engine.

Registered Users are provided with a *Personal Home Page* to store and manage customized alerts, searches, and links to favorite journals and articles. Additionally, Registered Users can view free Online Sample Issues and preview selected material from major reference works.

Licensed Customers are entitled to access full-text journal articles in PDF, with select journals also offering full-text HTML.

How do I become an Authorized User?

Authorized Users are individuals authorized by a paying Customer to have access to the journals in Wiley InterScience. For example, a university that subscribes to Wiley journals is considered to be the Customer. Faculty, staff and students authorized by the university to have access to those journals in Wiley InterScience are Authorized Users. Users should contact their Library for information on which Wiley journals they have access to in Wiley InterScience.

ASK YOUR INSTITUTION ABOUT WILEY INTERSCIENCE TODAY!